Columns

Of

Democracy

Also by Nicholas Johnson . . .

Test Pattern for Living (3rd edition, Lulu Press, 2013)

How to Talk Back to Your Television Set (3rd and 4th editions, Lulu Press and Amazon Kindle, 2013)

From DC to Iowa: 2012 (Lulu Press, 2012)

Predicting Our Future Cyberlife: 1970-2040 (Lulu Press, 2012)

What Do You Mean and How Do You Know: An Antidote for the Language That Does Our Thinking for Us (Lulu Press, 2009)

Virtualosity: Eight Students in Search of Cyberlaw (Lulu Press, 2009)

Are We There Yet? Reflections on Politics in America (Lulu Press, 2008)

Your Second Priority: A Former FCC Commissioner Speaks Out (Lulu Press, 2008)

Columns of Democracy

Nicholas Johnson

Lulu Press
Morrisville, North Carolina
July 2018

First Edition
Copyright 2018 by Nicholas Johnson

ISBN: 978-1-387-91129-5

With thanks to:

Mary Vasey – my wife, my life, my love – and retired English teacher; any errors are the result of not following her advice.

Gregory Johnson – AboutGregJohnson.com – my son and tech guru, without whose creativity and skills this book would have had neither covers nor formatting.

The editors and syndicates along the way, beginning in 1982 with the Iowa City Press-Citizen, followed by the Gannett, Register and Tribune, Cowles, and King Features syndicates. See https://tinyurl.com/ydduzq78.

More recently, including the columns in this collection, most were published in The Gazette, Iowa City Press-Citizen, and occasionally The Daily Iowan.

Currently I'm indebted to The Gazette's Todd Dorman, Lynda Waddington, and previously Jennifer Hemmingsen, for their encouragement, spirit, and editorial fixes. Following Gannett's cutbacks, Katie Brumbeloe has been skillfully and kindly playing all the parts at the Iowa City Press-Citizen. Without them all I could offer you would have been the blog, FromDC2Iowa.blogspot.com.

Table of Contents

Introduction 1

Chapter One /Democracy 17

    Defending Democracy 17

    Let's Seize Our Opportunity, Take Responsibility Seriously 20

    Include People in Process 23

    Focus on Our Common Values 25

    Public Comments About Public Comments Guidelines 26

Chapter Two/Education 31

    A. Higher Education 32

    What Is It With the Iowa State Board of Regents?! 32

    What Putin Can Teach Rastetter 35

    Better Ways to Pick a New UI President 37

    Parallels Between School Systems Are Staggering 40

    Regents' Multi-Million-Dollar Unused Asset 43

    Public Universities Not Using Radio Well 45

    Will Germany's Economic Formula Work for Iowa? 47

i

Can Biz Leaders Save Education?........................50
Saving Higher Ed; Step1: Listen to What Iowans Want..52
B. Beer and Football..56
Re: 21-Ordinance is Human-Rights Violation 56
Bars, Students Should Be Thankful 58
NFL Football: It's Only Television........................60
Let's Stop Making Players Pretend to Be Students 62
Should Sports Allow Drugs that Enhance Performance? 65
Enhancing Everyone's Experience at Kinnick...68
C. K-12..71
Is Superintendent Criticism "Defamation"? 72
A Win-Win Advisory Board for District...............73

Chapter Three/Policy 77
"Never Happen Again" Is Not Enough 77
Create a Caring Community 79
Building Consensus on Iowa City's Vision, Future 82
Design Communities to Support Communication, Interaction and Learning 85
Cancer: "Of Course; But Maybe".........................87
Recognizing and Reducing Racism....................90
Health Care, Housing Rights?............................93
Curbing Waste: Bad News, Good News 95

Some Basic Facts About Water 98
Working Our Way Through the McGinness Kerfluffle 100

Chapter Four/Politics 103
When Believing Is Seeing 104
Senate Ignoring the People's Voice 106
Trump Might Not Be Blundering in Race 110
Republicans Need to Get Their Party Back From Trump 112
Sanders the Right Democrat for Caucus 115
Throgmorton Is City Treasure 118
Re-elect Rettig for Supe, She Knows What She's Doing 119

Chapter Five/Taxes 121
Decisions Must Come Before Taxes 121
Congress' First Step in Long Journey 124
On the Local Option Sales Tax, Think Before You Vote 126
Think Long and Hard Before Diluting the Gasoline Tax 129
Like Death and Taxes, TIFs and TIFing Seem Here to Stay 131
TIF: If You Can't Beat 'Em, Insist on More Transparency 134
Too Many Negatives, Too Little Upside to TIFs 137

Talking TIF: Costs Outweigh Possible Benefits 138

Sycamore TIF Unnecessary 142

City is Putting Lipstick on TIFs 143

Vote "No" on Justice Center, But "Yes" for Courthouse 144

Getting To "Yes" by By Voting "No" on Justice Center 147

Still Many More Options for Jail 150

Residents Deserve Courthouse Annex 151

Chapter Six/Technology 153

Why Net Neutrality is Our Friend 153

Is Texting the Problem, or Just Part of the Problem? 155

Chapter Seven/War 159

The Militarization of America 159

Spending on Military Always Comes at a Cost 163

Is War the Best Answer? 165

Six Step Program for Avoiding War 167

Syria's Refugees: Job One and Job Two 170

Sober Risk Assessment Needed to Respond to Terror 173

What Motivates "Terrorist Thugs"? 176

Focus on Muslims Misplaced After Shooting .. 179

Is Boston Bomber's Photo Worth 11,000 Words? 182

About the Author **185**
Cover Photo Credits **187**
Index **189**

Introduction

War Then. I was seven years old on a cloudy, Iowa winter's day. The lazy Sunday afternoon offered neither plans nor inspiration. I was lying on the maroon carpet next to our Sears Silvertone console with AM and shortwave radio and automatic 78-rpm record changer and player. With a hearing loss that almost put me in the Iowa School for the Deaf, my head was buried in the cloth-covered speaker.

My six-foot-three father towered over me, holding the family's globe of the world.

It was December 7, 1941, and the announcer was talking about an attack by Japanese war planes against the Pearl Harbor Navy base on the Hawaiian island of Oahu.

Dad looked down to judge my mood and then sat on the floor beside me. Holding the globe in his lap, he placed the index finger of his left hand on Oahu and the index finger of his right hand on Iowa. It was his way of reassuring me the war was far away and that I was safe – though at that moment his concern probably exceeded my own.

After all, "war," especially inside America, was beyond my experience or even imagination. He, by contrast, lived through the build-up to World War I (1914-1918) and would have been 12 when American soldiers entered Europe prior to the end of that war. (The Armistice was signed November 11, 1918.)

The next day, December 8th, 1941, Congress passed a Declaration of War with Japan – as required by Article I, Section 8, Clause 11 of the Constitution.

Six months later the first contingent of future Navy pilots was housed and training at Iowa City's U.S. Navy Pre-Flight Training School. It was on a part of the University of Iowa campus two blocks from my home.

Less than four years later the war was over. Democracy had triumphed over totalitarianism.

"War" Now. On September 11, 2001, the attack on the Twin Towers destroyed both towers, killed 3,000 and injured 6,000.

There are few if any similarities between World War II and what happened next in 2001 – our current "war on terror."

Then we knew who our enemies were: Germany, Japan and Italy. They were countries. Japan attacked our homeland. Now enemies are usually not countries. Saudis financed and executed 9/11. We didn't retaliate with attacks on Saudi Arabia. Our government even allowed Saudis a rapid departure from the U.S. following 9/11. Instead we started military actions in Iraq and Afghanistan (neither of which attacked our homeland) – at best an odd choice.

Then we had a constitutional Declaration of War. Now Congress has failed to provide Declarations of War against any of seven countries with conflicts involving U.S. military (Afghanistan, Iraq, Libya, Niger, Somalia, Syria, Yemen).

Then the global World War II was won in four years. Now the "wars" in Afghanistan and Iraq are taking 17 years and counting (and there are U.S. military in 150 countries).

Then, 12 percent of Americans were drafted into the military. Every adult and child played a part. The

Vietnam War had draftees – and protesters. Now, the draft has been abolished; only 0.4 percent serve; we're shopping. There's no longer a reason to protest wars.

Then the cost of World War II was $341 billion. Now the post 9/11 cost of our military may be as much as $6 trillion, counting expenditures for the Defense Department, Energy Department (nuclear weapons), Veterans Affairs (lifetime healthcare for wounded), and interest on an increased national debt.

Then Americans believed they should give what they could to finance wars on a pay-as-you-go basis. With individuals' median annual income at $2,000, over 85 million adults and children (more than 50% of the population) bought $185.7 billion worth of War Bonds. Now we've gone shopping and put the cost of war on our children's and grandchildren's credit card. Then (1946) the national debt was $270 billion. Now (2018) it is $21 trillion with 2020 estimates of $24 trillion.

Then war consisted of unprovoked attacks by one country on another, military personnel of two or more countries each dressed in distinctive uniforms, using conventional military weapons (rifles, grenades, tanks), fighting over territory and a shifting frontline. Now our "war on terrorism" does not involve a prior attack by a country on our homeland, is often a war of choice, not defined by countries' borders, in which our "enemy" refuses to wear identifiable uniforms and looks like our allies and innocent civilians, fighting with homemade "improvised explosive devices" rather than planes and tanks. There is no frontline, because this is not really a fight over territory. When the going gets tough the terrorists just move operations to another country containing Americans they can attack.

The goal of terrorism is terror. Letter bombs, pressure cooker bombs, cars driven into crowds, and mass shootings have increased children's nightmares and adults' terror. Our response? Billions spent on "security." But why are these attacks only terrorism when done by Muslim immigrants? What of identical attacks done by American-born Christians?

Moreover, our costly responses always seem to be one step behind. One guy got on a plane with a bomb in his athletic shoe and years later millions of airline passengers were still required to remove their shoes – which did little to protect 23,000 runners in athletic shoes when two pressure cooker bombs exploded near the 2013 Boston Marathon finish line.

We have also been a little slow to recognize the terrorists' shift to weapons called computers in a war fought on a battlefield called the Internet.

Indeed, it was only this year (2018) that the Defense Department elevated the cyber domain to a fully recognized combatant command: Cybercom.

Sadly, we're still one step behind. Yes, our enemies are still developing software capable of bringing down our electric power grid, acquiring classified military documents and corporate collections of personal data on millions of Americans.

Yes, we have not adjusted well to how "wars" are now fought. We are still spending trillions of taxpayers' dollars on World War II weapons such as multi-million-dollar fighter planes and multi-billion-dollar aircraft carriers.

Global War on Democracies. But as serious as all of this is, it pales in comparison with America's greatest threat – the global war on democracy and human rights.

For decades a central element of our foreign relations has involved support for democracies and human rights where they exist, and their encouragement where they do not. Despite recent cutbacks in the State Department's budgets and personnel it still contains a Bureau of Democracy, Human Rights, and Labor.

A Pew Research Center 38-country survey late last year found that over half the population in each country consider democracy a very, or somewhat, good way to govern. https://tinyurl.com/yaa48fma. Confronted by Pew pollsters with the alternatives of rule by the military, strong leaders, or experts, those with greater education and wealth were more likely than others to favor democracy. Sweden's citizens ranked it highest, followed by those in a group of countries including Australia, Canada, Germany, Greece, Netherlands, and the U.S. However, Pew's results also noted that "a deepening anxiety about the future of democracy around the world has spread over the past few years."

The 2017 Planet Rulers list of "Current Heads of State & Dictators" identifies 49 "current world dictators and authoritarian regimes." All are presumably unsettled by U.S. support for democratic institutions and human rights.

The State Department's 2013 Russia Country Report on Human Rights alleged that Vladimir Putin's Russia "continued its crackdown on dissent, ...

discriminated against LGBT persons, ... [and] had yet to bring to justice the individuals responsible for the deaths of prominent journalists, activists, and whistleblowers." In addition, there were "allegations of torture and excessive force by law enforcement officials, life-threatening prison conditions, interference in the judiciary and the right to a fair trial, restrictions on freedom of speech and press, ... electoral irregularities, widespread corruption, societal and official intimidation of civil society and labor activists, violence against women ... and limitations on workers' rights."

It's only natural Russian President Vladimir Putin would want to see cuts in the U.S. State Department's budget and personnel, and an American diplomacy bereft of a democracy and human rights agenda – as began after January 2017. Leaders with practices like Russia's undoubtedly shared Putin's delight with these changes in our State Department.

It's tempting to label such countries' leaders as dictators, fascists, strongmen, or totalitarians. But such labels can create backlash, merely intensifying followers' commitment to, and defense of, their leader.

Better than to utter opinions, generalizations, or conclusions dipped in slur words is to merely describe as factually as possible not what those leaders and governments "are" but what they are "doing."

Non-Democratic Countries' Practices. So, what are they doing?

Personal Power. A central feature is such leaders' accumulation of personal power over their government's institutions, their people, and among the world's nations.

After WW II President Truman and others created the United Nations, Marshall Plan, World Bank, and NATO – then thought to be in our own national interest. There were coalitions of democratic nations. Today's non-democratic leaders seek the disintegration and destruction of such coalitions of democracies.

Propaganda. A non-democratic leader replaces independent mass media with propaganda praising the leader and eliminating criticism. This may include personal or government ownership of broadcasting and newspapers, intimidation and punishment of owners and journalists (including assassination), criticism to erode the public's trust in and reliance upon mass media (an "enemy of the people"), or blocking external broadcast signals, Internet sites, and publications.

Shifting Responsibility. Responsibility for any shortcomings in the economy and citizens' lives is shifted to "the other" – liberals, political opponents, African-Americans, immigrants, Muslims, elites, and Jews. The leader seeks to divide the nation by increasing existing divisiveness – what Tom Lehrer observed in the song, "National Brotherhood Week."

Oh, the white folks hate the black folks,
And the black folks hate the white folks. ...
The poor folks hate the rich folks,
And the rich folks hate the poor folks. ...
And the Hindus hate the Muslims,
And everybody hates the Jews.

Projections of Strength. The projection of strength takes many forms, from control of the military, threats of its use, toleration and even encouragement of a tough police state and thuggery to bragging and exhibition of the leader's personal physique.

Disempowerment of Opponents. There may be disparagement and disempowerment of opponents (including imprisonment and assassination), an extension of the leader's term of office (sometimes as long as a lifetime), and interference in or even elimination of free and fair elections. It may include everything from discouraging voting (identity cards, short hours, long lines), to threats and intimidation of supporters who don't vote and opponents who do, to redrawing voting district lines (gerrymandering), or overt corruption (ballot stuffing).

Legislative Control. A related effort will address control over elected legislative bodies – after acquiring sufficient personal political support from the leader's base to nominate and elect a legislative majority or even dissolve the body when thought necessary.

Judiciary. A law of rulers will replace a rule of law. The judiciary and rule of law could otherwise operate as a check on executive abuses. This can take the form of eroding public trust in, corruption of, or total control over the judiciary (such as executive appointment and removal of judges.).

Education. Educational institutions may also pose a threat to the leader. Citizens with a college education may be more willing to question authority, express dissent, and join organizations of opponents. Academics and research scientists may reach conclusions that challenge the leader's ideology. One response is attacking academics as biased, unpatriotic elites. Another response is to cut school budgets, raise tuition, close schools, or discourage the education of women.

The Big Lie. Supporting each of these efforts is the leader's ability to lie, continuously and effectively. Whoever said, "the first casualty of war is truth" might well have added and "the first casualty of lying is democracy." What's effective lying? As Hitler's Joseph Goebbels counseled his leader, "If you repeat a lie often enough, people will believe it."

Kleptocratic Oligarchy. As an anonymous eighteenth-century English verse put it:
The Law doth punish the Man or Woman
Who Steals the Goose from off the Common
But lets the greater Felon loose
That steals the Common from the Goose
Another of non-democracies' qualities is often the leader's quest for personal financial enrichment as well as financial gain for a circle of his or her friends and supporters: a kleptocratic oligarchy.

Evaluation of President Donald Trump by these standards – his campaign, followers, administration, words and action during the past three years – will be left to the reader. And we must acknowledge that any attacks on our own democracy are as much the responsibility of the voters as their elected officials.

Americans Accepting Democracy's Alternatives. Reference to the Pew Survey, above, emphasized the proportion of the population of democratic countries that supports governance by a representative democracy. What is possibly of equal or greater concern are the percentages of Americans who believe nondemocratic alternatives "would be a good way to govern our country": governance by a strong leader

(22%), the military (17%), or "rule by experts" (40%).

It would be exceedingly foolish to ignore the signs the attacks on the columns of our democracy (such as an independent media, rule of law, and public education) are increasing. They come from within and without, while a large proportion of our fellow citizens are unaware, apathetic, or supportive of these trends.

But it would be overly pessimistic to fail to see, acknowledge, and participate in the opportunities for civic engagement that remain. Democracy is studied, applied, enhanced (or ignored) first and foremost in our own hometowns – as de Tocqueville discovered and wrote in *Democracy in America* in 1835. Each community has its own strengths and challenges.

This book of columns represents one person's use of one of the columns of democracy: a free and independent press. Some columns in this book deal with democratic institutions, others with subjects that may relate to your community. All are illustrations of what this column of democracy looks like.

My hometown, Iowa City, Iowa, is a college town, home to the University of Iowa, a major research university and medical center. In addition, local manufacturers shipped nearly $3 billion of product in 2012. The population of 74,000 (2016) is 24% non-white, 14% foreign born; 95% have a high school diploma, and 60% have a B.A. degree or higher. Median income, 2012-2016, was about $43,000.

The politics are sufficiently progressive that many Iowans refer to Johnson County (Iowa City is the county seat) as "The Peoples' Republic of Johnson County." Because of Iowa's early caucuses in presidential years, any resident who wants to can meet and question the candidates – one of whom may end up president of the United States. Sadly, the political enthusiasm this generates is not transferred to extraordinary numbers of registered voters or their turnout in school board, city council, and county board of supervisors elections.

Iowa City is blessed with three newspapers: The Daily Iowan (student paper), The Gazette (employee owned), and Iowa City Press-Citizen (Gannett chain). All welcome readers' proposed columns and letters to the editor; many are published (but of course not all). The 64 columns organized between these covers represent one example of what it was still possible to have published in the heartland of America 2013-2017.

Chapters deal with such columns of democracy as education, public policy issues, politics, taxes, technology and war – each subject is deserving of public attention and debate in a democratic society.

Rather than introduce or summarize the content of each column, the reader is referred to the introductory material preceding each chapter, the table of contents and fulsome index.

Our Alternatives. Which brings us to the status quo – sometimes defined as "the mess we're in now." Have we no option other than to sit and watch the waning of democracy in our country and abroad, as we might watch a waning moon cross the sky?

There are two categories of alternatives. But neither is easy. Both require our commitment, courage, imagination, time, and occasionally money.

The first requires awareness of a truth propounded by Frederick Douglass:

Power concedes nothing without a demand. It never did and it never will. Find out just what any people will quietly submit to and you have found out the exact measure of injustice and wrong which will be imposed upon them, and these will continue till they are resisted with either words or blows, or with both. The limits of tyrants are prescribed by the endurance of those whom they oppress.

Frederick Douglass, "West India Emancipation" speech, Canandaigua, New York, August 3, 1857.

The response to this awareness need not involve violence; indeed, it can often produce better results if it is peaceful.

To stay on course requires a concise and clear statement of specific grievances and solutions.

Demands may utilize massive marches or demonstrations in the streets and outside elected officials' offices. They may include a membership organization, signatures on petitions, picket signs, TV and newspaper advertisements, billboards, street theater, presentations to organizations, door knocking – the only limits are common sense and the imaginations of participants.

The other approach is to rachet up one's personal participation in such of the former columns of democracy as may remain – because you can, it will make a difference, make you feel better and be an example for others. These are things each of us can do on our own.

What are they?

Political participation. Make sure you are

registered to vote, know the location of your polling place, have whatever identification is required, vote in every election, and encourage others to do so.

Discover the local impediments to voting. Explore ways of eliminating those impediments, including solutions other communities have found successful.

Register with, and offer to work for, a political party. Most need precinct workers – even precinct captains. Volunteer to work for candidates pledged to rebuild our columns of democracy.

Consider running for office – starting with the local school board, city council, county board of supervisors, or state legislature. If that sounds daunting find a local board or commission you can join.

Mass media. Our nation's newspapers, on average, have lost half the subscribers and advertising dollars they once had. The local news necessary to sustain a democracy is at risk in many communities. Subscribe to your local paper, at least the digital edition.

Know Your Agencies and Issues. Develop at least a nodding acquaintance with your community's challenges and public agencies. Select an issue you will follow closely. Consider adopting the local agency primarily responsible for that issue. Attend its meetings and get to know the members and employees.

Use Public Media. If the paper isn't covering your agency thoroughly, consider starting a blog in which you report and comment on your agency's doings. Turn blog posts into letters to the editor and columns submitted to the local paper. Become available for radio and TV interviews.

Education. Read up on democracy; ask your

librarian to recommend basic documents and books. (While you're there, ask if they could use a helping hand and if their budget has been cut.) Attend relevant public lectures; maybe take a course.

Talk to your children, friends, and others about democracy and dictatorships, the history and qualities of each, and why you prefer the former. Find out how much the social studies teachers in your local schools are providing students regarding democracy and current attacks upon it – what used to be called civics.

Public education is one of the essential columns of democracy. Find out how supportive your local community and state are of K-12 and higher education. Are the budgets are up or down? How do they compare with those of other cities and states? Is the local college or university headed by a business person with few if any academic credentials? Is it replacing tenured faculty with part time adjuncts and raising tuition to levels that exclude many students? Are there tuition-free community colleges?

Judiciary. Are state and local judges elected? Are appointments partisan, or do they reflect bar associations' evaluations of nominees' competence? How long are judges' terms? Is there evidence of potential conflicts of interest from campaign contributions? Do powerful political or economic forces influence the laws affecting judicial process?

Diversity. Is your community welcoming to immigrants and refugees? Are systemic racism and sexism seemingly everywhere? What is your community doing about it? Is your police department attempting to improve police-community relations?

What programs or activities bring the community together? Is local income inequality taken into consideration in balancing city revenue from property taxes and sales taxes? Are there segments of the population in need of additional social services, such as housing, nutrition, healthcare and transportation? These are issues of relevance to democracy.

It is said that as Benjamin Franklin was leaving the Constitutional Convention he was approached by a man who asked, "Well, Mr. Franklin, what kind of a government did you give us? A Republic or a Monarchy?" To which Franklin replied, "A Republic – if you can keep it."

For 230 years we did keep it. American democracy confronted challenges along the way, but none succeeded in abolishing democracy. From the time I first thought about such matters at the age of seven (December 7, 1941) the possibility we would not keep it never entered my mind.

Then my father was able to reassure me that America's democracy would survive a traditional World War II. Today's attacks on the columns of democracy are in many ways more invisible, invidious and destructive than those from Japanese fighter planes and bombs in 1941. Can we give our children and grandchildren a reassurance similar to what my father provided me 77 years ago – reassurance that American democracy will survive?

Not now.

What the future holds is up to us.

Chapter One /Democracy

Introduction

During the years these columns were written there were signs of increasing stress on American democracy: declines in civics education, legislatures' funding of K-12 and higher education, percentages of eligible voters who register and vote, households with newspaper subscriptions, and civil discussions of policy differences. The columns in this chapter address various aspects of democracy.

Defending Democracy
The Gazette, December 3, 2017, p. C4

> *Don't it always seem to go*
> *That you don't know what you've got*
> *'Til it's gone*
>
> – Joni Mitchell, "Big Yellow Taxi"

There are many divisive issues these days: climate change, renewable fuels, perpetual war, health care, tax reform, higher education, trade policy. The list seems endless.

However, most agree on preserving democracy's fundamental pillars: free speech, public education, voting rights, and an independent judiciary.

Presidents Thomas Jefferson and James Madison offered us insights.

Media. Jefferson wrote, "were it left to me to decide whether we should have a government without newspapers, or newspapers without a government, I should not hesitate a moment to prefer the latter."

Media are one of the few industries expressly protected by the Constitution (First Amendment). They were to serve all the people, expose abuses by the powerful, and create a "marketplace of ideas" from which "truth" would emerge. There would be no central control of media by either government or big business.

Americans' 19th Century "Internet," their "social media," was transportation – rivers, roads, a transcontinental railroad, and pony express. Our "e-mail" was their postal mail. Low postal rates encouraged the distribution of books, magazines and newspapers.

For the FCC to repeal Net Neutrality, ownership limits, and the Fairness Doctrine, or for politicians to say media are "the enemy of the American people," chops away at one of democracy's pillars. (Now 46% of voters believe media make up anti-Trump stories.)

Free public education and libraries. Jefferson continued, "But I should mean that every [person] should receive those [newspapers] and be capable of reading them." In his epitaph, he chose to be remembered as "Father of the University of Virginia" – omitting any reference to his presidency.

Madison agreed: "a people who mean to be their own Governors, must arm themselves with the power which knowledge gives."

Free public schools would enable citizens to

inform themselves. Free public libraries would provide every American access to the information resources of kings.

When legislatures don't fully fund public universities, adding to the trillion-dollar debt of graduates, they are undercutting democracy's pillar of "free public education." This not only hampers America's ability to compete with the nations that do provide tuition-free college, it also strikes a blow against democracy.

Voting rights. Over time, the opportunity to vote – a democracy fundamental – was expanded from white, male, landowners over 21 to everyone over 18.

State legislatures that pass laws making it more difficult, rather than easier, for all to vote, or that draw district lines enabling a minority of voters to elect a majority of their representatives, are attacking a democracy fundamental.

Independent judiciary. The founders created a respected, independent branch of government, the judiciary, as a constitutional check on Congress and the executive branch. Federal judges' independence was protected by their lifetime appointments. Justice would be delivered under a "rule of law" rather than a law of rulers.

To disparage the judiciary, charging bias, or lack of competence, to appoint those unqualified, weakens a democracy's last, best protection of our civil rights.

We can probably survive most wrongheaded public policies. What our democracy can't survive are attacks on its fundamental pillars. Let's defend what we've got before it's gone.

Let's Seize Our Opportunity, Take Responsibility Seriously
The Gazette, November 22, 2015, p. C3

The following text was submitted to The Gazette as a part of one of its "Writers Circle" projects, this one focused on "voting." Portions removed for the hard copy published version are included here and enclosed [in brackets].

> *I am waiting for someone
> to really discover America . . . .*
>
> – Lawrence Ferlinghetti, "I Am Waiting," A Coney Island of the Mind (1958)

      On November 3 Iowa City held an election of city council members. The somewhat unique existence of two slates of candidates, whose differences over issues were clearly drawn, might have produced a massive voter turnout. It did not.

      Approximately 62,000 Iowa City residents are eligible to register as voters. Of that number only 45,000 do so (72 percent). But wait; it gets worse. In the latest city council election only 15 percent of those who bothered to register also bothered to vote.

      My Oxford English Dictionary (1971) defines "democracy" as "that form of government in which the sovereign power resides in the people as a whole and is exercised either directly by them or by officers elected by them. In modern use often more vaguely denoting a social state, in which all have equal rights, without hereditary or arbitrary differences of rank or privilege."

Has America ever had such a democracy? Does it have one now?

We believe we can bring "nation-building" to others, showing them the virtues of our democracy. But it is they who assume the risks associated with voting, including in some instances death, stand in long lines for hours, and emerge from the polls with a proud smile and a finger painted purple.

Meanwhile, many Americans stay at home with their TV sets and video games on Election Day, only to have their faces turn purple months later as they rail against the evils of ["guv-ment" (in quotes) was deleted and "government" was substituted].

Fact is, our nation began, not as a democracy, but as the plutocracy it remains today. As Noam Chomsky reminds us, it was John Jay who proclaimed that "those who own the country ought to govern it."

To insure this result, voters were initially limited to males who were white, over 21, and owned land. This has been gradually expanded to include African Americans, those without land, women, and finally all over 18. Thus, those who own the country today have to govern it by choosing the nominees.

[William "Boss" Tweed, of New York's 19th Century Tammany Hall, is credited with having said, "I don't care who does the electing, so long as I get to do the nominating." Today the nominating takes place in New York's financial district, Wall Street, well to the south of the old Tammany Hall at 141 E. 14th Street. As Goldman Sachs' CEO Lloyd Blankfein and his friends have said privately about Hillary Clinton and Jeb Bush, echoing Boss Tweed, "Those would be two very good choices and we'd be perfectly happy with them."]

[But if the American poor, working poor, working class, and lower middle class were well informed regarding their interests, registered, and then voted as a block, they could put their candidates in every elected position in the country, from school boards to the White House. That's why it's so important for the 1%, even though they do the nominating, to put every possible roadblock in the path of the poor on their way to the voting booth – with schemes only restrained by the limits of their imagination.]

[And that is why the establishment's two major parties make it virtually impossible for third parties to rise and survive. Proposals like instant runoff, fusion, and many more, would make it possible for us to vote with both our hearts and our heads – better reflecting Americans' true preferences, while leaving the two parties dominant. But the two majors generally succeed in keeping third party candidates from even being seen in the national debates.]

[Asked to delete or substitute something for the above paragraph, I proposed, and The Gazette used:] Voting reforms such as instant-runoff, ranked choice, or preferential voting would enable voters to vote for more than one candidate. Voting with both one's heart and head would better reflect Americans' true preferences. It also would breathe life into third parties, now usually excluded from participation by a Commission on Presidential Debates made up of the Democratic and Republican Parties' leadership.

Iowans are blessed with laws and practices encouraging, rather than stifling, registration and voting. We are given the heady responsibility of playing a disproportionate role in the nomination of our presidential candidates. If anyone will ever "really discover America" it will probably be right here in Iowa. But only if we'll take our responsibilities seriously and use the opportunities we have.

Include People in Process
The Gazette, July 24, 2106, p. D3

I started life in a house on the former underground railroad, in an Iowa City with "northern racism" – few black students and fewer professors, none of whom could find a barber to cut their hair, or a landlord to rent them an apartment.

I spent the 1950s in a Texas with "southern racism" – including the poll tax and other remnants of slavery those underground travelers escaped. I clerked for a federal court of appeals judge when civil rights decisions sparked burning crosses in judges' yards.

Later, as a President Lyndon Johnson appointee, I watched how he passed the Voting Rights Act, knowing it would hand the South to the Republicans.

And how, as a result of that act, the mud and gravel roads in southern black neighborhoods began to be paved. The number of southern black legislators increased from 5 to 313.

Those memories came back to me as I read that

Cedar Rapids' leaders had met regarding a sub-set of local gun violence that gets little public or media attention: young black gang members shooting each other.

Ultimately, those leaders created the Safe, Equitable and Thriving (SET) Communities Task Force.

Wisely, the members chose to focus, not merely upon the existence and consequences of these shootings, but upon their causes. They mentioned "poverty, social vulnerabilities, and other systemic hardships."

Having done so, they realized their challenge is less about race relations (though that's involved) than about the basic needs of all residents – a challenge confronting most American cities.

The usual approach lists things like jobs at livable wages, housing, transportation, and health care – noting their interrelationship. Three weeks ago this paper addressed the adverse effect on education from both inadequate housing (in an editorial) and insufficient transportation (in a column).

Perhaps our answer this time will be found, not alone in substance (like housing proposals) but in process. The Task Force might first find the problems by focusing on those most impacted by what Cedar Rapids lacks (for them), rather than those most benefited by what it has. It might focus more on listening to their stories, recording and reporting anecdotal evidence, than on cold data and multiple choice questions.

What if identifying each individual's problems came before those of the community, a search through the catalog of alternative solutions, pilot projects, and the difficult task of final implementation?

We might just find that, like Lawrence Ferlinghetti, we, too, have been "waiting for someone/to really discover America," and that our democracy requires more than voting. It needs citizens who feel, and are, included in the identification as well as the resolution of our challenges.

Indeed, our leaders might wish to meditate upon Lao Tsu's 2500-year-old observation that the goal of a good leader is that "When his work is done [the people] will say, 'We did this ourselves.'"

Iowa City now has less "northern racism." And Cedar Rapids can have less shooting by gang members. We can do it. But only when the people can say, "We did this ourselves."

Focus on Our Common Values
The Gazette, January 1, 2017, p. D2

The prefix, "comm," has been around for 700 years: "communication," "the commons," a "commune," "communitarian," "communal" – and "community." My column in this space last year focused on the role of communications in defining and building a community.

This year's focus is on our common values; the standards we want for all.

A couple weeks ago, in a play based on Dickens' A Christmas Carol, I played Mr. Fezziwig – a jolly employer with communal values, in stark contrast to their absence in Ebenezer Scrooge. It is a contrast, alas, that persists 170 years later.

Eastern Iowa, and this newspaper, are blessed with a good many Fezziwigs. My suggestion for 2017 is that we come together in the spirit of the United Nations' Universal Declaration of Human Rights to draft our own (see especially Articles 25 and 26 – look it up).

What do we wish for all who live among us? We are all in need of something. Even the well-educated wealthy can suffer disabilities or addictions. But what can we do for those with less income, new immigrants, recently released prisoners, homeless veterans, or those with jobs but no reliable transportation?

A "community" should know, and implement, the answers.

Public Comments About Public Comments Guidelines
Iowa City Press-Citizen, February 15, 2014

The Iowa City Community School Board commendably, endeavors to govern through enunciated policies. But sparks flew at Tuesday's meeting during the public's comments about public comments guidelines from the board.

Let's put the issues in context.

1. "Open Meetings" don't require "open mikes." The law requires the school board to permit the public to attend its meetings (subject to specific exceptions). It does not require the board to permit the public to

speak at those meetings.

2. Board members are volunteers. They have limited time to tend to the board business the law requires they address in open board meetings. Doing that business is the meetings' primary purpose.

3. The board needs stakeholder input. There are many reasons why. (a) It is of the essence of a self-governing democracy that students, parents, teachers and others be heard. (b) Elected officials are responsible to constituents. (c) Board members' decisions should be informed (though not dictated) by public comments – especially when an agenda item has limited prior opportunity for public input.

4. We need "public citizens." Journalists can't do it all. The public would be better off if all school boards, city councils, county boards and legislative committees had a few people following their work like our school board does. You don't have to approve all of their tactics to know that the board and public would be worse off without our public citizens' research and tenacity. In fact, think about picking your own agency to track.

5. Alternative opportunities. Input's not limited to meetings. Consider talking to board members, sending them email or letters. The board might have a website to display public comments and interactive listening sessions. If board members' responses reflect occasional modifications of prior positions, these alternatives can reduce (though not eliminate) the need and desire for discussion during board meetings.

6. The guidelines. There were two categories of public objection to the guidelines: some involved

specific language, others a "slippery slope" concern of greater restrictions to come.

(a) School boards, like legislative committees and judges, have the inherent right, and responsibility, to maintain decorum in their workplace. Judges don't need detailed regulations; an ignored warning risks contempt of court. School boards can't fine or jail for disruptive behavior, but they can apply common sense – and even remove individuals if necessary.

(b) Guidelines' language should be sufficiently precise to be clear without excessive detail. Even Iowa's first speed limits were simply "reasonable and proper."

(c) Allowing public comment at the beginning of meetings, rather than at the end, is just plain thoughtful. As for time, the board could declare that time for comments, in total and for each speaker, will vary depending on the number of people who want to speak, how often that speaker has spoken, the public interest in a topic, and the amount of board business.

(d) Having speakers sign in, speak one at a time, and from the podium, can promote order and improve television coverage.

(e) Avoid vague standards regarding the content of speakers' statements. Saying comments must involve "matters of public concern," expressed with "respect and decorum" is both too narrow and overly broad. The same can be said for the guidelines' specificity regarding punishments for violations. Certainly, speakers should not be prohibited from criticizing the board and administration, or for using occasionally colorful language. Some content-based restrictions could even run afoul of the First Amendment.

This challenge can be met. In the end, it is a matter of balance and common sense – something for which Iowans are noted.

30 – Columns of Democracy

Chapter Two/Education

Introduction

I come by my interest in education naturally. My mother was a school teacher, my father a university professor. My first "school" was participation in the Iowa Child Welfare Research Station's two, three, and four-year-old groups. That was followed by K-12 years in the University of Iowa's experimental schools, University Elementary and High School (closed in 1972 and now named "North Hall"). Our teachers were university professors developing national tests and research-based teaching methods.

Two years out of law school (University of Texas, Austin) I was back in a law school classroom as an associate professor (University of California, Berkeley). In 1980, upon my return from Washington to my hometown, Iowa City, I was invited to teach at the University of Iowa's College of Law (until retirement in 2014). From 1999 to 2002 I also served on the school board of the Iowa City Community School District and wrote a biweekly column about K-12 education for the Iowa City Press-Citizen.

Thus, it is not surprising that I am both a strong supporter of education (as one of the columns of democracy) and a sometimes critic as well.

A. Higher Education

What Is It With the Iowa State Board of Regents?!
Iowa City Press-Citizen, May 16 2014, p. A7

What is it with the Regents and the University of Iowa?

An earlier Board ran off one of the most competent university presidents in the nation, who was quite willing to stay. (He had to settle on the presidency of one of the nation's most prestigious universities at three times the salary. He's now president of the Smithsonian Institution.)

The Register editorialized March 8 that, "The Iowa Board of Regents took [UI President] Sally Mason to the woodshed last week" for lack of communication – when it was they who cancelled the meetings she had requested.

Later that month, believing this efficient and innovative University needs to be more so, it hands over $2.5 million to a consultant. "UI Says, 'Deloitted to Meet You,'" https://tinyurl.com/y825bj6x.

There are many descriptions of consultants. I've always liked, "Consultants borrow your watch, tell you the time, then walk off with your watch." Doesn't the University of Iowa have comparable resources?

In their latest episode of "Can You Top This?" the Board has a committee proposing a new "budget formula" to transfer money away from the University of

Iowa to Iowa State and the University of Northern Iowa. Although the Board refuses to release the proposal, the Register reports [May 6] the formula funds graduate and professional students equally with undergraduates, and only funds students from Iowa.

Memories of Peter Yarrow's March 9 Englert Theater rendition of "when will they ever learn" flows "gentle on my mind."

As soon as I heard the May 5th news of this latest IED the Regents left along the road to Iowa City, I laid out some of its problems in "Iowa's Economic Foundation? Graduate Education & Research," http://fromdc2iowa.blogspot.com/2014/05/iowas-economic-foundation-graduate.html.

The short answer, of course, is that graduate and professional education cost much more per student than undergraduate education. For example, California's "budget formula" appropriates five times as much for each dental student as for undergraduates.

Later, former Dean Gary Fethke added supporting detail of these cost disparities ("Regent System Shouldn't Be One-Size-Fits-All," May 10), followed by 13 former Faculty Senate presidents' letter.

The proposal will necessitate reducing the quantity and quality of education received by Iowans (and others) at the University (including undergraduates). But its negative impact will not be limited to the UI's students, staff and faculty. It will harm all Iowans by, among other things, reducing the University's economic contribution to Iowa's economy – currently roughly $6 billion a year.

What else is wrong with this proposal?

The adage is right: "You get what you measure." The proposal bases UI's share of appropriations on Iowans, without regard to their disparate costs of education. That's an incentive to compete for undergraduate Iowans by lowering admission standards, minimize the number of professional and graduate students, and turn away the international and out-of-state students who actually pay higher tuition. Why reject that 40% of non-residents who choose to come to, and then stay in, Iowa?

Besides, exposure to a wide variety of individuals is a significant part of a young Iowan's education at our universities. Students from other countries and regions of our country, various socioeconomic levels, different races, ethnicities and languages, among other things, enrich education.

In addition to the UI's $6 billion contribution, what Iowa's economy needs is not only more jobs, but more UI grads who can create jobs, and fill those going wanting for lack of highly-skilled applicants.

Major grants go to top research universities. The UI is one of them. To continue as such it needs to attract, and hold, top faculty. The near-half-billion UI receives in research grants is not inevitable. A funding formula that ignores this income is a foot shooting exercise.

Regents, however you feel about the University of Iowa, consider Iowa's economy. Graduate and professional education is its foundation.

What Putin Can Teach Rastetter
The Daily Iowan, May 6, 2016, p. 4

Regents' President Bruce Rastetter appears to need some mentoring regarding the democratic dialogue between the state's Board of Regents and the stakeholders of Iowa's state universities – namely, all Iowans.

It might be too much of a shock to start with examples from the world's great democracies, such as the British House of Commons Question Time, or President Obama's "We the People Petitions." That would be like Rastetter running naked from a Finnish sauna and jumping into a frigid snow bank. No, it's best he begin with baby steps.

Perhaps he should start by studying the "formerly communist" countries.

Russian President Vladimir Putin spent his 20s and 30s with the KGB. Rastetter could begin by aspiring to achieve Putin's style of democratic dialogue. So how does this major country's leader, this Donald Trump enthusiast since December 2015, the fellow whose attack jets flew at 500 mph near sea level and within feet of a U.S. Navy destroyer April 11 and 12, how did he go about a dialogue with his people two days later?

As the New York Times reported, Putin's "live call-in show [ran] three hours and 40 minutes ... [Q]uestions poured in about high prices, unpaid wages, rising utility bills, and the closing of schools and hospitals. In all, around 3 million questions . . .."

From the opening question, this was no nine-inning softball game. Putin acknowledged how many questions dealt with poor roads. Indeed, the first questioner showed a video of traffic on her roads, complained about the abundance of potholes and even got in some licks about the lack of sidewalks and bicycle paths.

As for Putin's responsiveness, Rastetter might want to note the Times report that "after the first caller [from Omsk] complained about the poor state of the roads there, the city posted on Twitter pictures of new asphalt being laid down before Mr. Putin was off the air."

There are a couple other things Rastetter might discuss with President Putin.

One is the tuition-free university education Russia provides its students and how Iowa might join this expanding group of progressive states and nations. (Russia has the highest percentage of college-educated citizens in the world.)

The other is how Putin gained a firmer grasp of American politics than Rastetter – who put his money (literally and figuratively) on New Jersey Gov. Chris Christie. In December, President Putin had perceived Trump (whom he's praised) as the candidate most likely to win the Republican nomination.

In summary, both Putin and Rastetter take questions from constituents. But there the similarity ends.

Putin takes the questions of greatest concern to Russians and answers or otherwise responds to them. Iowans get no responses; it's not clear the regents even watch their video comments.

Putin gave the exchange nearly four hours, on

nationwide television, during convenient times for viewers, in which he was an active participant. Rastetter devotes one hour, during times least likely to encourage participation, in which no regent participates.

Putin receives 3 million questions from 143 million people. A comparable goal for Rastetter, based on Iowa's population, would be 60,000 inquiries from Iowans.

Hopefully, of course, Rastetter will soon be able to far exceed these minimalist communist standards.

Better Ways to Pick a New UI President
The Gazette, September 27, 2015, p. C5

Iowa Board of Regents President Bruce Rastetter says those objecting to his selection of Bruce Harreld as the University of Iowa's next president "embrace the status quo of the past over opportunities for the future and focus their efforts on resistance to change instead of working together to make the UI even greater."

Which would be worse: that he truly believes this, and is unaware of the rational objections to his process and choice, or that he has deliberately chosen to divert the public's gaze away from his actions?

Since Harreld's selection I've encountered no one who advocated UI's personnel should "embrace the status quo." Why would anyone reject "opportunities for the future" to become "even greater"?

If it looks, walks and quacks like a duck, it's

probably a duck. And this one has looked, walked and quacked like a done deal since July. That's when special treatment began for Harreld and his wife by the UI's interim president and search committee chair, Regents' president, and Governor Terry Branstad. The waste of money, people's time, and embarrassment to legitimate candidates was significant. Legally, the Regents could have just picked Harreld in July – or brought four business persons to campus.

Chief executives of Yahoo, Radio Shack, Bausch & Lomb, and a Notre Dame football coach were fired for falsifying their resumes. Harreld falsified his. Either the Regents failed to vet, or just didn't care. Harreld had zero academic administrative experience. His business record was mixed. He had never served as a Fortune 500 corporate CEO or governor. His public forum performance was embarrassing.

Those are a few of the understandable reasons for the negative response, and why it's inaccurate, insulting, and duplicitous to suggest it was just academics' desire to "embrace the status quo."

Did the Regents deliberately set out to make it virtually impossible for any president to succeed, by destroying the trust faculty representatives had been building? If so, they could not have chosen a better process and candidate.

So here we are. If Harreld does not resign, if the Regents win legal challenges to their process, if the University does not lose its accreditation along with its reputation, what are our next steps?

Governor Branstad was a founding member of ALEC, a Koch brothers-funded right-wing organization writing, lobbying for, and enacting states' legislation promoting the ideology of privatization and corporatization. ALEC has its own higher education agenda.

Those who wish to attack public higher education, or "transition" it to something else, deserve to be heard – but only if they will talk.

So let's start with specifics. What exactly do Rastetter and the Governor want from Harreld's "transitioning" the University?

Tenure, like lifetime appointments for judges, has been a centerpiece of the academy's integrity. Increasingly, students are taught by untenured adjuncts. Do they want to do away with tenure entirely?

Do they want to apply profit-center analysis to class size, favoring 500-student lecture halls, or classes of 100,000 online students?

Is their education-for-jobs preference so great that they want to diminish or eliminate, UI's College of Liberal Arts and Sciences?

When policy is driven by ideology, rather than history and data, it can produce an ISIS-like destruction of a society's greatest treasures. And "the university," as an idea in virtually all nations and cultures, with its evolution over the millennia, is as worthy of protection from ideologically-driven destruction as Iraq's antiquities.

It can be helpful for any organization to reassess its mission and performance from time to time – including the Board of Regents, given how far it has strayed from conventional board governance principles.

It's also true for American higher education in general, and the University of Iowa in particular – all of which are already doing exactly that.

But there are some preliminary steps before picking a new institutional leader with "experience in transitioning other large enterprises through change," as Rastetter characterizes Harreld's qualification.

It's necessary to begin by (1) involving all interested parties in an evolving consensus regarding, (2) an assessment of performance compared with output goals (*e.g.*, what knowledge and skills do we want our graduates to have?), (3) identifying what may need changing, (4) what changes have already come about over the last 20 years, (5) researching what comparable institutions are doing in this country and abroad, (6) prioritizing what most needs doing, and (7) designing and testing some pilot projects.

Then pick the president.

Watch this space.

Parallels Between School Systems Are Staggering
Iowa City Press-Citizen, November 10, 2015, p. A5

Once upon a time, a Midwest university's governing board hired a president who was a lifelong business person with no advanced degrees, record of scholarship or political experience. They cited his "business acumen" as sufficient qualification – over faculty protests. He had worked for IBM in sales and ultimately as vice president. He then became a business consultant, and headed a corporation no longer operating under that name.

He froze faculty salaries, except for a favored few (without explanation), and scaled back graduate assistants' tuition waivers and health insurance subsidies, just hours before fall classes began. He discontinued clinical privileges for a Planned Parenthood physician and terminated relationships with Planned Parenthood affiliates.

This is not a once-upon-a-time bedtime story. It's a true tale. But it doesn't involve Iowa's Bruce Harreld.

It's a Missouri story. The state's multi-campus system is headed by a president, the campuses by chancellors, all governed by a Board of Curators.

The current dustup is at the university in Columbia and involves the president's insensitivity to the grievances of African-American students regarding racial epithets and worse. It wasn't something he said. It was that he said nothing.

Realizing that nothing gets an administrator's attention like loss of revenue, especially from sports, the football team announced it would boycott all "football related activities" until President Timothy M. Wolfe resigned or was removed. Serious at any time, it was especially so before the BYU game November 14, to be held in the Kansas City Chiefs' stadium. If the game was forfeited, the university would not only lose ticket and related revenue, it would owe BYU $1,000,000. The coaches and others on campus supported the team.

A half hour after I began writing this column the Board of Curators called an emergency meeting, and twenty minutes after that Wolfe resigned.

(For a similar story about a business person as president of Iowa's Parsons College, and its ultimate bankruptcy, see Laura Crossett's "Parsons College: A Cautionary Tale for UI," https://tinyurl.com/y9m3wy88.)

Since September 1 I have been maintaining a repository of the news, opinion pieces and documents relevant to the Board of Regents' process, and ultimate selection, of our new president. See tinyurl.com/qfok7f6 and tinyurl.com/phpuvl4.

These records are important, not only to us, as University of Iowa news for today and as an archive of Harreld's presidency for tomorrow. What is going on in Iowa this year is but one part, one story, of what is happening in higher education all across America – as illustrated by the news from Missouri. It is far too early for historians' evaluation of whether the "business person" solution preferred by many boards will turn out to be the salvation of challenged universities, or lead to their demise – or to know how many historians will then remain to tell the tale.

Nor is this story limited to our nations' major research institutions. It is but a part of trends throughout our society during the past 35 years. Grover Norquist put it succinctly: "I don't want to abolish government. I simply want to reduce it to the size where I can . . . drown it in the bathtub." We're witnessing public support for outsiders as presidents of the United States as well as its universities.

Privatize prisons and their profits are tied to

maintaining the world's largest prison population. Privatize the military, pay contractors multiples more than soldiers, and we have perpetual wars. Bust unions in the private and public sectors and the middle class disappears and increased wealth goes to the top 1%. Repeal Glass-Steagall and taxpayers bail out the banks.

Corporatize the universities and . . . what? Watch this space.

Regents' Multi-Million-Dollar Unused Asset
Iowa City Press-Citizen (Online), June 8, 2013

The request was for "a short column providing advice for the newly appointed regents for how to be effective in their new role."

It's not that I haven't studied, experienced, and written about board governance – visit https://www.nicholasjohnson.org/governance/. It's that, given these regents' experience, they are hopefully already seeped in the governance literature.

So instead, here's some free advice, worth every penny, regarding regents' effectiveness with a major substantive challenge.

When I was a member of the University of California, Berkeley, Law School faculty, public higher education meant near-free college education for students at a University of California, a California State

University, or California Community College. The state's percentage of post-high school educated was almost twice Iowa's.

This was not unrelated to California's rapidly growing economy – then among the world's top seven, had California been a country.

Roughly three-fourths of Iowa's adults do not have a college degree. It's understandable that they would have little interest in, and less understanding of, the importance of our public universities to every resident.

One of our public universities' greatest challenges is helping every Iowan, including legislators, understand the bargain represented by public support for education. As the bumper sticker has it, "If you think education is expensive, try paying for ignorance."

Ironically, the regents control a statewide multi-million-dollar media network that is used almost not at all for this purpose: Iowa Public Radio (which the regents just acknowledged is a governmental institution).

I'm not suggesting the regents' stations broadcast nothing but classroom lectures. But the schools have a half-dozen or more stories every week, distributed to, but seldom used by the mainstream media, that could help build public understanding. Some could be one-minute items during program breaks; others five-minute radio news segments or entire programs.

Iowa's distinguished Professor Jerald L. Schnoor has been doing this. But he had to find a network of 200 commercial stations to carry his programs, rather than IPR.

Ideally, I'd like to see program series teaming local officials with university experts on such things as local water quality, flooding, tourism, K-12 education, health care delivery – whatever Iowa's communities would find most helpful.

There are lots more programming ideas in "Self Help for a Helpful University," http://fromdc2iowa.blogspot.com/2013/03/self-help-for-helpful-university.html, and its links.

As a former FCC commissioner, I can assure you regents that when the FCC gave you broadcast licenses we assumed you knew they were only available for "educational" purposes.

Public Universities Not Using Radio Well
The Gazette, March 28, 2013, p. A5

As a law professor with administrative law focus, Diane Heldt's well written "IPR Not a Government Body" story, March 26, offers me a delicious final exam essay question.

As a former FCC commissioner, I see more here than Iowa's open meetings and public records laws.

There's a reason why Iowa's public universities hold licenses to this multi-million-dollar statewide network.

Frieda Hennock, the FCC's first woman commissioner, set aside the low FM frequencies for noncommercial "educational" stations.

Today's Iowa Public Radio is neither noncommercial nor educational. Indeed, it's baffling why schools that think they're misunderstood don't use this valuable resource to tell their story. "Self Help for a Helpful University," http://fromdc2iowa.blogspot.com/2013/03/self-help-for-helpful-university.html.

I'll leave the legal opinions to others but running commercials on a station licensed as noncommercial isn't the only problem.

If the universities want to fritter away what their stations could contribute to the schools' mission, that's one thing. But if IPR is truly "not a government body," and a part of neither the Regents nor the state schools, there is, minimally, at least an ethical and moral issue as to whether the schools should continue to hold their valuable licenses to these "educational" stations.

In sum, the remaining issues are: (1) is the delegation of station operation from the state's universities and their Board of Regents to Iowa Public Radio consistent with the spirit behind the initial grant of "non-commercial, educational radio" licenses by the FCC to these universities; (2) how much more problematical does this become if IPR does not consider itself a subsidiary unit of either the actual license holders or their Board of Regents; (3) if IPR is, as its attorney insists, "not a government body," then what is it; (4) how can IPR's provision of time during program breaks to for-profit entities to promote their businesses, in exchange for cash, and stimulating this revenue stream by on-air promotions emphasizing the business benefits to advertisers from doing so, be considered "non-commercial" just because they call it "underwriting" ("if it looks, walks, and quacks like a duck"); and (5) why are the universities so reluctant to put their own "commercials" on their own stations, similar to the examples provided in "Self Help for a Helpful University"?

If I ever come across responses, let alone "answers," to any of these questions you'll be the first to know.

Will Germany's Economic Formula Work for Iowa?
Iowa City Press-Citizen, January 16, 2015, p. A7

The Iowa Legislature and Board of Regents emphasize college education for Iowans – at least those whose parents can afford the tuition, or graduates accepting debt with their diploma. Others debate pros and cons of extending 12 years of free public education to 14 ("Too Good to Be True? Time Will Tell on Tuition Plan," Iowa City Press-Citizen, Jan. 14, 2015, https://tinyurl.com/yclm6bk7).

Meanwhile, Germany is only the latest country to realize that free higher education for all world citizens promotes economic growth in each of its states ("Länder"). Other countries with similar programs include Brazil, Finland, France, Norway, Slovenia and Sweden.

Humboldt-Universität in Berlin is one of the most prestigious universities in Europe and has educated 29

Nobel Prize winners. Many of these "international universities" offer their free courses in English as well as the native language – although improving one's foreign language is one of the benefits of study abroad.

Tennessee is leading the trend in the U.S. with free community college education. Chicago is among the first big cities. President Obama is urging all states to follow.

As an educator, I'd like to believe this movement reflects a simultaneous epiphany among the world's public officials regarding the many values of a liberal arts education. Have they at last come to see that quality education, like universal single-payer health care, is a basic human right (Universal Declaration of Human Rights, Arts. 25 and 26)?

Alas, that's not the case. Providing free college education to all, like the free food samples at Costco, is just good business.

Germany is part of a global economy. The more world citizens with German ties, the more the Länders' economies grow. It's true whether students from abroad stay or return home with networks of German contacts. It's equally true of German students otherwise without access to higher education. The German economy benefits when they stay; it benefits when they study abroad, stay, and do business from there.

Iowa, unlike Germany does not grasp this simple truth. Our leaders believe if Washington can pay for a war with tax cuts, Iowa can create prosperity with tax cuts. Both Washington and Des Moines are in desperate need of remedial math.

Iowa Workforce Development has warned of our

challenge "to overcome a skills gap." We don't have a shortage of jobs, we have a shortage of middle and higher skilled workers. Our state universities don't have too many students from abroad and out of state, we have too few. Too few Iowans who have studied abroad and stayed there to help develop markets for Iowa products. Too few from abroad who have studied here and stayed here – or gone back home with ties to Iowa businesses

This is not rocket science. There's data. There's history. America and Iowa enjoyed an economic boom during the 1950s. Major contributors were the 2.2 million returning veterans of World War II who received a free college education under the GI Bill. California's growth from a destination for Dust Bowl immigrants in the 1930s to one of the world's 10 largest economic powers in the 1960s is directly linked to its deliberate economic policy of free higher education. New York's is, in part, a similar story.

Iowa can't gamble its way to prosperity. It can't build a growing economy on tax cuts. It can't sustain economic growth by bribing fickle out-of-state businesses to locate here.

What it can do is look to the history of the World War II GI Bill, and the growth of California. What it can do is try to understand the rationale behind Germany's policy of free education for all. What it can do is, like President Obama, follow a progressive state like Tennessee and city like Chicago.

Will it work for us? Let's think it through.

It would require the uncommon political courage of deferred gratification: putting Iowa's long-term economic growth above Iowans' short-term economic greed. And, yes, it requires a willingness to raise and invest taxes. But that educational investment could prove to be much more profitable than using taxpayers' money to bribe out-of-state corporations, or as paybacks to major campaign contributors.

Can Biz Leaders Save Education?
The Gazette, Insight, August 22, 2017, p. A6

How can we get legislative funding for all Iowans' post-high-school education?

Aside from bemoaning tuition increases – before increasing tuition once again – those responsible have shown little sympathy and less results: state university presidents, Board of Regents, Gov. Kim Reynolds, and legislators.

Where can we turn?

How about those who hold political power and control: the business community?

Business leaders are assuming more social and political responsibility. When many Republican leaders did a little sidestep around President Donald Trump's seeming tolerance of neo-Nazis, CEOs of large corporations resigned from Trump's business councils in protest. A similarly prestigious group of corporate leaders defeated the Texas legislators' "bathroom bill." Many business owners are making sure their employees will have health care.

Might they lobby for education appropriations as

well?

An educated population benefits everyone – and business most of all. Iowa's problem is not a shortage of jobs. It is a shortage of skilled workers (as well as entrepreneurs and a creative class). More skilled workers mean less turnover and training, improved productivity, quality control, profits, and economic growth for Iowa's towns.

Business leaders are aware the post-World War II economic boom was driven by a college-educated workforce of veterans, paid for by the GI Bill. California and New York built comparable economic growth with decades of tuition-free higher education. Globally, business leaders in 24 countries are benefiting from employees with tuition-free college educations; 13 of those countries offer tuition-free educations to other countries' students as well (including ours).

Historically, Iowans willingly have financed public education since the first one-room schoolhouse in 1830. By 1910, the state was one of the first with a statewide high school system, until recently ranked one of the country's best.

After another 107 years, expanding public education from K-12 to K-14 is scarcely a premature, radical move. Rules vary, but nine states already have some form of tuition-free community college: Arkansas, California (San Francisco), Louisiana, Minnesota, New York (plus four-year college), Oregon, Rhode Island, South Dakota, and Tennessee.

Expanding such a program to the three, four-year regents universities (as New York has done) might be premature. But starting with Iowa's 15 community colleges ought to be possible.

If Iowa wants to build a competitive edge in a global economy, it must first construct the educational foundation to support it. It simply can't afford to leave qualified, willing students uneducated.

Business leaders: Legislators look to you for ideas as well as campaign contributions. You can give them a nudge, give them permission, you can insist they fund at least tuition-free public community colleges for Iowans.

Indeed, if you don't insist, it will never happen.

Do it for your business, your shareholders, your town, your family – or because you know it's the right thing to do. Just do it.

Saving Higher Ed; Step1: Listen to What Iowans Want
The Gazette, March 19, 2017, p. D1

As a child of the University of Iowa – literally and figuratively – its current financial woes are troubling.

Frankly, I don't think the Iowa Legislature can pass the laugh test when it awards $12 billion in tax breaks while fashioning a $7 billion state budget and then says it "can't afford" to adequately fund its "state" universities. The truth? It just has other priorities.

What to do?

The American Academy of Arts & Sciences recommends its Lincoln Project's "An Educational Compact for the 21st Century" (http://tinyurl.com/

hk59pq9). It's not the first proposal for our plight and won't be the last – but it's at least coherent and data driven.

On March 9, the Academy organized a powerhouse panel in Iowa City (and later Des Moines) to discuss this Compact. It was headed by the project's co-chair, Mary Sue Coleman, President, Association of American Universities, and former president of the Universities of Iowa and Michigan. Joining her were UI President Bruce Harreld and former University of Illinois Chancellor Phyllis Wise.

Our multi-faceted Jim Leach added to the panel his experience as our former member of Congress, Chair of the National Endowment for the Humanities, and currently UI's Senior Scholar, Chair in Public Affairs, Professor of Law, and Interim Director, Museum of Art.

It turns out that Iowa's woes are part of a national trend. States' support of research universities declined 35% the last 17 years (per full-time student, in constant dollars). Private universities have three-to-four times state schools' funding per student. We can hope for a brighter future, but as President Harreld said, "Hope is not a strategy. We may need a 'Plan B.'"

There's more to the Educational Compact than a column can hold: the impact of research universities' discoveries on Iowa's (and the world's) economic growth and job creation (the purchases of a mere eight schools put $2 billion into 1750 counties one year), their research that corporations can't or won't do, their advances in medical science, their innovative cost-cutting efforts, the economic as well as personal value from arts and humanities (Jim Leach's HUMANISTEAM), or their financial aid for low income undergrads, among many others.

The tuition-free college programs of California and New York – and the one in the post-World War II GI Bill – were a major reason for those states, and our nation's, spurts of economic growth.

But if that evidence isn't enough, how can legislators be persuaded?

President Harreld came the closest with his insightful, joking (and illegal) proposal for a vote-buying, pro-education PAC.

There's another Politics 101 approach that never came up; something I've been harping on for years and was reminded of November 8, 2016.

In 1936 President Roosevelt won by over 24% (61% to Alf Landon's 36%). The coalition that made that victory possible – the unemployed, working poor, working class, and ultimately union members – held for 40 years. When the Democratic Party started turning to Wall Street and corporations for the money, and the East and Left coasts for the voters, it lost its natural constituency along with its soul – a constituency that, had it been served, could have assured victories in every election from school boards to White House.

For higher ed to restore its state funding it needs the support of legislators; to have the support of legislators requires the support of their constituents. Higher ed has been as neglectful of its constituents as the Democrats have been of theirs.

Historically, Iowans' enthusiasm and generosity for education has been overwhelming. It still could be.

In the 1800s they paid for 12,000 one-room schoolhouses for their kids. In the 1900s they were rightfully proud of funding a K-12 system ranked among the nation's best. Iowa State University began in 1858, was aided by President Lincoln's Morrill Act of 1862, and "focused on the ideals that higher education should be accessible to all." But it, the University of Iowa, 1847, and University of Northern Iowa, 1876, were primarily built with Iowans' dollars, further evidence of Iowans' continuing financial commitment to these educational ideals.

It's clear why businesses in Ames, Cedar Falls, and Iowa City, should support the Regents' universities. But why should the residents of Iowa's 96 other counties? How can we answer their question, as President Harreld posed it, "What have you done for us lately?"

We have answers: Where do you think your agricultural research, doctors, nurses, and teachers come from? (http://tinyurl.com/hrf9wwb; click on any county.)

But what if they don't have those doctors, our graduates aren't their kids, and our astrophysicists' discoveries haven't touched their lives?

Let's start by asking, "What do Iowans most want in their communities?" Then let's shut up and listen, rather than telling them how great we are. As President Harreld said, "We can't just wait for the people to come; we need to reach out. We owe the public something back."

We've taken baby steps in that direction. I went on two of what are now called the University of Iowa

Engagement Tours – Iowa professors travelling by bus, discovering our beautiful state, meeting with local leaders.

OK. But what we most need is at least a ten-fold expansion of what the UI calls our "Outreach" program. (http://tinyurl.com/j64swh5.) We need to listen to the legislators' constituents, then survey the universities' resources to see what we could do, as their responsive partners, to help solve their communities' problems or flesh out their proposals.

Iowa Public Radio, the multi-million-dollar statewide radio network, licensed to Iowa's universities, could be a big assist with this effort.

We don't need another bus ride. What we need is a "full Grassley" of 99 counties with an army of listeners.

The rule in Washington is that you do ten favors for a politician before you ask for one in return. The same applies to universities' constituents. What collaborative favors have we done for Iowa's communities lately?

This political approach will take time, yes, but it's legal, will cost a lot less, and produce a lot more, than that PAC.

B. Beer and Football

Re: 21-Ordinance is Human-Rights Violation
The Daily Iowan, October 17, 2013, p. A4

There are all kinds of age-based laws and regulations restricting those underage from, among other things, getting married, driving cars, buying guns, performing in porn videos, purchasing cigarettes – and yes, buying alcohol. None is considered a human rights violation. See, "Deeth's Drinking Age: A Reply," https://tinyurl.com/y97lhbfj.

Bars are in the business of profiting from the sale of alcohol. Those under 21 are legally prohibited from buying, possessing or consuming alcohol. The logical and most easily administered standard would be to prohibit anyone under 21 from ever entering a bar – as is the standard in many places.

Instead, Iowa City lives with a compromise that both enables bar owners to profit maximize, and underage students to be in bars for 20 out of every 24 hours each day. Those under 21 are only kept out of bars from 10 p.m. to 2 a.m. Supporters of this hypocrisy have the nerve to call it "21-only"!

It seems to me the City Council's approach is exceedingly generous to bar owners and their illegal binge-drinking students, not something either should be protesting.

And since the author [John Deeth] raised the "no one over 50 in bars after 10" example, nor is it a denial of my human rights as an old geezer that I must get my driver's license renewed more often than my middle-aged children do. Someday it may be forcefully taken from me. The state has a right to determine if my driving puts at risk my own safety and that of others.

As John Neff has noted in a comment on the blog essay linked above, "The age dependence of hazardous use of alcohol decreases much faster than a Constant/Age with most of the problems in the 15 to 25 age range. The peak age is about 19, so 21 is a reasonable compromise for the minimum legal age to drink." In short, that's why the legal drinking age is 21. It, like limitations on my driving, is designed to minimize the risk of harm underage drinkers pose to themselves and others.

Meanwhile, 21 remains the legal drinking age. John Deeth has endeavored (earlier on these pages and elsewhere) to make the case for lowering the drinking age to 18. But until he persuades the Congress and Iowa Legislature of his position, (1) keeping those under 21 out of bars is logical, (2) permitting them in bars until 10 p.m. is generous, and (3) leaving them there until 2 a.m. is just asking for trouble – the trouble we got the last time we tried.

Bars, Students Should Be Thankful
Iowa City Press-Citizen, November 3, 2013, p. A8

Bars are in the business of profiting from the sale of alcohol. Those under 21 are legally prohibited from buying, possessing, or consuming alcohol. The most logical and easily administered standard would be to keep those under 21 from entering bars, as is done elsewhere.

Instead, Iowa City enables bar owners to profit maximize, and those who cannot legally purchase alcohol to be in their bars 20 hours a day. They are excluded only from 10 p.m. to 2 a.m. It's scarcely "21-only."

Our City Council's approach is exceedingly generous to bar owners and their student customers alike, something for which they should be grateful rather than protesting.

To keep the underage, all-but-four-hours-a-day bar access, you vote "No." To repeal it you vote "Yes." So voters may be confused. They may not even vote. But few are undecided.

So why write more?

Because there are a couple of really bizarre bits of rhetoric the controversy has inspired that need examination.

One is that people who are legally precluded from purchasing what a business is selling are thereby somehow deprived of their "human rights." They say it's a similar violation to exclude them from bars during the four hours when they cause the most mischief.

There are all kinds of laws restricting those underage from, among other things, getting married, driving cars, buying guns, performing in porn videos, purchasing cigarettes – and yes, alcohol. Never, before now, has any been considered a human rights violation.

The other is that because the drinking age should be 18, rather than 21, therefore it's OK for underage students to violate the law and drink alcohol. I follow that argument "all but the 'therefore.'"

Until opponents persuade the Legislature of their position, (1) keeping those under 21 out of bars is logical, (2) permitting them in bars until 10 p.m. is generous, and (3) leaving them there until 2 a.m. is just asking for trouble – the trouble we got the last time we tried it.

NFL Football: It's Only Television
The Gazette, January 18, 2015, p. C2

I can understand someone being a fan of high school football. Students know the players sitting with them in class. Parents come to the games. It's a community thing; a neighborly thing. Sometimes fans' enthusiasm gets a little out of hand, but mostly it falls short of physical violence and destruction of property.

Even small college football retains some of these qualities. Big money college sports? Not so much.

But NFL football? What is that all about?

Big money college football engages the pretense that players are "student-athletes." There's less hypocrisy in the NFL. It's big moneymaking commercial enterprise pure and simple. It does not even pretend to be anything else. Fans cannot possibly have any more emotional or nostalgic tie to their "local" NFL team than they would have to their local Ford dealer.

Think about it. With the exception of the community-owned Green Bay Packers, NFL teams are "owned" by someone, just like that Ford dealership is owned. Local citizens' tie to the team is primarily the contribution they made as taxpayers to building a multi-hundred-million-dollar stadium where the millionaire players of the billionaire owner stage some of the TV industry's most profitable programs.

Many NFL team owners, and most of the players, have no prior tie to the community. Few citizens have the sense of having grown up with them. Indeed, given the prices for skyboxes and tickets few citizens can afford to see those owners and players anywhere other than on a television screen.

Now don't get me wrong. I'll be watching Super Bowl XLIX along with the millions of my fellow Americans who will make it one of the highest rated TV programs in 2015. It's good television. In fact, as an FCC commissioner, ABC's football coverage struck me at the time as programming that most effectively optimizes television's technological potential.

It's live, unrehearsed, and unpredictable in outcome. It takes place within a defined area, permitting the positioning of lights, cameras, and mikes for optimized coverage and close-ups. The timeouts enable commercial breaks consistent with the programming. And it inspires the innovation of such features as instant replay, overhead cameras, digitally positioned scrimmage lines on the field, and other features that now include a virtual 3-D appearance on large, home screens.

And these games are just a TV show in another sense.

The NFL, as a television production company, is in many ways a single corporate entity. The players are only competitors for the time of the game on the field. To ensure that their competition is close enough to be attractive to audiences and advertisers, efforts are made to equalize the ability of those teams – through rules about the draft of new, replacement players (similar to "replacement smokers" for the tobacco industry), and the sharing of revenues.

The teams' owners are kind of board members of the parent corporation, the NFL. They make the rules and hire the CEO. The players are sometimes traded between teams, know each other, and often appear quite friendly to the "opposing" players. Yes, one team "lost" and the other "won" – but in reality, the players on both teams won a lifestyle otherwise unavailable to most of them.

So what is this fan loyalty about? I think it's embedded in our DNA. It's a carry-over from when our family loyalties extended to our tribes – tribes that still war in many parts of the world where the NFL has not yet offered an alternative. Without the NFL, if Americans really understood the income inequality from which they suffer we might have another American revolution. Without our tribal loyalties to NFL teams we might be inclined to start even more wars abroad.

So relax. Give thanks to the NFL. Enjoy the games. But if your favorite tribe loses, remember: It's not just "only a game." The reality is that "it's only a TV show."

Let's Stop Making Players Pretend to Be Students
Iowa City Press-Citizen, August 27, 2014, p. A11

Text that was submitted, and contained in the online version, but deleted from the hard copy edition is [in brackets].

John Dean, President Nixon's chief White House counsel, famously warned his boss in 1973 that the Watergate burglary was "a cancer growing on the presidency."

With the opening of the college football season, somebody needs to warn the presidents of big money football schools that there's a cancer growing on their presidency.

There have been earlier diagnoses of disease.

In 1906, when college football was killing 15 to 20 players a year, and permanently disabling 150 more, U.S. President Teddy Roosevelt told college presidents he'd outlaw the sport unless they made it safer. Reluctantly, they agreed to require helmets and organized what became today's NCAA.

University of Chicago President Robert Maynard Hutchins considered the team a distraction, scorned colleges that received more publicity from sports than educational programs, and with trustee support simply abolished football in 1939.

Hutchins' analysis and solution are even more persuasive today. But few politically perceptive football critics advocate the death penalty – nor do I. So long as parents and players know the health risks, taxpayers know the costs, fans know its cost in time and money, and all still want football, we'll have it.

Moreover, there is a win-win cure for this cancer that would solve current challenges confronting both higher education and big money college football.

The cancer has metastasized its conflicts of interest for everyone in higher education. University presidents find it easier to capitulate to coaches than fight (Penn State). Athletic directors must rationalize taking advertising and skybox dollars from the alcohol and gambling industries. [Coaches must encourage players' classroom performance, while their multi-million-dollar salaries turn on players' on-field performance. Non-tenured professors fear flunking players.] Players who do seek a college education must choose between lab time and scheduled practice.

Nor is the current system loved by the big money football programs.

The NCAA lives in a 1906 dream world peopled with academically accomplished students playing football without helmets just for fun, and the college professors who doubled as their volunteer coaches. This vision is an increasingly tough sell when the highest paid public employees in most states are college football coaches, and their college football industry grosses billions of dollars a year.

College players want to unionize, to be paid the full costs of attending college, and a share of the millions of dollars schools make from the players' likenesses in video games. They want reimbursement for the health care costs of football-related concussions and other injuries that may last a lifetime.

[Conferences are expanding. The once-midwest-centered Big "Ten" schools are now 14, including Penn State, Rutgers, and Maryland – well to the east of Iowa. The wealthiest football schools, and their conferences, have just negotiated a withdrawal from some of the

NCAA's restrictive regulations.]

[In short, this is not your great grandfather's college football.

What's the win-win cancer cure?

Recognize the big money college football programs for what they are – profit-making, commercial entertainment organizations, serving as farm clubs for the NFL (even if only 1.6 percent of college players will be NFL draftees), substantially disconnected from the research, scholarship, and classroom instruction of their schools.

Free them from NCAA regulations and their inherent conflicts. Remove the requirement players must pretend to be college students.

The rest is administrative detail. Most professional leagues already have provisions for players who've not attended college. Perhaps the football corporations could lease their former facilities (Kinnick Stadium) and name (Hawkeyes). Players who want an education might have a degree program permitting spring-semester-only enrollment.

When there is a win-win cure for a cancer of any kind, it's a shame to refuse even to talk about it.

Should Sports Allow Drugs that Enhance Performance?
The Gazette, August 17, 2016, p. 5A

I'm not proud to say it.
It was the 1960s. Illegal drugs were everywhere.

I was a young lawyer, living as a hippie-public official. That's what kept me from drugs – not health concerns, personal discipline, or common sense. Illegal drugs simply couldn't be part of my life.

That doesn't mean I'm a fan of our "War on Drugs."

Illegalization has promoted more crime, not less. It probably contributes even more deaths from drug dealers' use of guns than from their customers' use of drugs. Because there's no quality control of illegal drugs they're even more deadly. It's occasionally involved our government in the cocaine trade.

Not only has it cost taxpayers billions of dollars, it has deprived governments of the taxes on sales (like they get from sales of alcohol and tobacco).

When it rarely produces a dip in supply, that simply drives up street prices and profits for dealers. It's made us the number one nation for percentage of incarcerated citizens – including more blacks working as prison laborers today than once worked as slaves.

So what's the alternative?

In 2001, Portugal repealed criminal penalties for possession of marijuana, cocaine, and heroin. Fears of increased users' consumption and taxpayers' costs proved unwarranted. Health services for addicts were cheaper than incarceration. Teens' drug use and HIV from dirty needles declined. Addicts seeking treatment more than doubled.

Performance Enhancing Drugs (PED) – the elephant in the Rio Olympics' venues – brought Portugal's experience to mind.

Athletes' PED use began with the first Olympics

2000 years ago, 776-393 BC. Today it's present in most sports, from high school, to college, to the Olympics, to professional athletes. Efforts to stop it have proven as futile as our 1920s prohibition of alcohol, and more recent War on Drugs.

If only ineffective it would just be a waste of money. As it is, it also infuses otherwise honorable, sportsmanlike contests with subterfuge, lying, and deceit – to the harm of sports' fans, athletes, and our children. It risks athletes' health from the lack of physician monitoring and athletes' use of unsafe, untested substances and dosages. It encourages a contest of escalating sophistication in the design and detection of ever more difficult-to-detect substances.

Need athletes be protected from themselves? Injuries and death occur in many sports; athletes "assume the risk," legally and morally – think brain injuries from football. Shouldn't adults be as free to do their own benefit-cost risk assessments of doping as of any athletic or other risk?

Want a level playing field? It doesn't exist.

Many things can enhance performance. Athletic parents who start training their three-year-olds. Poor students who have to run five or ten miles each way to school. Wealthy parents who provide private coaching and clubs, and free their college athletes from the need to work. Coaches with the equipment and knowledge of sports science (including diets) to maximize training efficiency. Working out at higher altitudes to gain an oxygen boost upon return.

Doping also can and does affect performance. But because it is also illegal, surreptitious, and widespread, it creates a terrible conflict for coaches and athletes – dope and risk getting caught or comply with the rules and risk adding the hundredths of a second that can separate winners from losers.

Perhaps organized athletics, including the Olympics, should consider abandoning their ineffective anti-doping efforts. Perhaps they should consider the sports equivalent of the Portugal approach. Let doping join the long list of other things by which athletes and coaches can enhance performance – with approved drugs, dosages, and supervision by medical doctors and pharmacists.

A perfect solution? Of course not. But with a 2000-year history of failed bans, it may be a least-worst option worth trying.

Given today's widespread doping in all sports, the competitive results would be little different. But it would be safer, less deceitful, and create a more honorable and level playing field for athletes, coaches, and fans alike.

Enhancing Everyone's Experience at Kinnick
Iowa City Press-Citizen, April 29, 2015, p. A13

During a previous life, the University of Iowa's athletic director set about enhancing fans' "game day experience" at Wyoming Cowboys' football games.

He bar-coded tickets and opened more stadium

gates to speed entry. He provided parking lots and shuttle services – with discounts for flying the Cowboys' flag. He added 75 parking spaces for fans with disabilities. He improved restrooms and concession facilities. Solid improvements.

Flash forward to Iowa's Hawkeyes.

Well below national averages, only 64 percent of Iowa's season ticket holders are even "likely" to renew. Of those not renewing, 68 percent have concluded that seven opportunities to watch Hawkeyes lose too many games (while fans sit unprotected in Iowa's weather) is not a sufficient benefit to justify the cost: $790 for a couple's season tickets – plus their added costs and hassles of attending.

When the fast-food hamburger chains see a decline in sales, they have a five-step program to increase sales. First, they add salt. If that's not enough, they add sugar. Next, cheese. Then two burgers per bun. If none of that works, there's the nuclear option: bacon in everything.

AD Gary Barta is evolving his own multi-step program. When too many of the 70,000-plus seats in Kinnick Stadium were empty, he tried luring fans with a sound system, then a video board. He acknowledged both needed work and discovered neither filled the seats. Neither did the $70 discounts on concessions for early renewal.

What bacon on burgers is for McDonald's, alcohol is for Hawkeye football, a liquid lariat from Laramie for roping and corralling fans into Kinnick. Once praised for offering those with disabilities more parking spaces, he has now grasped the revelation from Ogden Nash's two-line poem that "Candy is dandy/but liquor is quicker." He's extended the hours for tailgate drinking and booked two night games – his way of "enhancing the game day experience" for Iowans.

That is, enhancing fans' memories of the party while forgetting the game. The theory? The more they drink, the more they party. The more they party, the more they forget what they were doing before they passed out. The more they forget the losses, the more they renew season tickets.

Of course, the most effective food and football solutions in providing customer satisfaction and enhanced game days? Better beef in hamburgers, and winning seasons for the Hawkeyes.

So how to win? The problem is not with the athletic director, coaching staff and athletes. They're entitled to our sympathy. The problems with big money college football are systemic.

College football needs to take some lessons from the National Football League for which they are the farm teams.

For starters, college ball, like the NFL, needs to be split off from academic institutions. Trust me; it would make it easier for everyone – university presidents, faculty, staff, students, coaches, athletes, sports writers, broadcasters, advertisers, investors, sports gamblers and fans.

Examples?

First, Barta notes that stadium beer sales "potentially could be a big revenue stream," but that's not now possible. Also, because of the university affiliation, the commercial ties between the football program and Riverside gambling casino are both a violation of the spirit of NCAA regulations and an academic embarrassment.

Second, the teams need to recognize that, like the NFL, college ball is a single industry in which every team's income would increase if talent were more equally distributed. They need a draft, in which teams with the poorest records get the best new players.

Third, the Iowa Hawkeyes play in Iowa weather. Kinnick, wedged between a railroad track, an expanding hospital and residential neighborhoods, was great in the 1920s. Today? Not so much. The team needs a domed stadium, with plenty of parking, preferably centrally located among eastern Iowa's population centers.

More alcohol (Barta's "fun factor") impacts Kinnick's neighbors. Parachuting 60,000 to 70,000 uninvited visitors into a neighborhood designed for 250 people, give or take, shifts football's costs to the neighbors. Students urinating in residents' yards, breaking glass beer bottles into shards, throwing trash under bushes isn't "Iowa nice."

These three proposals could truly enhance everyone's game day experience.

C. K-12

Note: Although only two columns from 2013-2018 dealt in some way with K-12 education, as noted in the Introduction to this chapter, "From 1999 to 2002 I served on the Iowa City Community School District

School Board and wrote a K-12 column for the Press-Citizen every two weeks." Those columns are accessible from my Website, http://www.nicholasjohnson.org.

Is Superintendent Criticism "Defamation"?
Iowa City Press-Citizen, June 28, 2017, p. 7A

There's a local issue regarding limits on citizens' criticism of school superintendents. Can the critics be sued for defamation?

I won't take sides on whether the criticism is arranted. Moreover, social norms may be more relevant than "the law." In either case, one's reputation is a thing of value.

Not all criticism is defamatory. There must be an unambiguous, clearly false, factual statement (not just opinion), that causes measurable harm to one's reputation among a relevant group (such as potential employers or customers).

The false assertion that a superintendent stole $97,000 from the schools' playground fund could be defamation. Saying, "I think he's doing a lousy job" would not be.

Moreover, the Supreme Court has ruled that while citizen plaintiffs need only show falsity, public officials must prove "that the statement was made ... with knowledge that it was false or with reckless disregard of whether it was false or not." Why? Because protection of political speech lies at the heart of First

Amendment guarantees.

As Justice Brennan wrote in New York Times v. Sullivan, "[we have] a profound national commitment to the principle that debate on public issues should be uninhibited, robust, and wide-open, and that it may well include vehement, caustic, and sometimes unpleasantly sharp attacks on government and public officials."

This is for newspaper readers only, not legal advice. If you're involved in a defamation case, get a lawyer.

A Win-Win Advisory Board for District
Iowa City Press-Citizen, September 5, 2013, p.A7

Be sure to vote Tuesday for Iowa City Community School Board.

OK; but for whom?

We are blessed with this year's offering: nine good choices. Each brings at least one quality that would benefit our board.

Study what the Press-Citizen brings us about them. There may be reasons for your preferences.

If you want a steady-as-she-goes board member – responsive to community pressure, soft spoken, able, collaborative – some candidates' training and experience suggests they might be, by your standards, marginally preferable to others.

If you want a shake-'em-up board member –

innovative, constructively abrasive, researching and advocating best practices, willing to take on the administration and special interests – you may find others marginally preferable.

If you think, however significant the district's challenges and opportunities may be, the first task before taking up that agenda is for board members to understand board governance – the role of a board members and their interaction with the administration – there may be others who appeal to you.

But there's no bad vote; no candidate who needs to be avoided at all costs.

When I was a School Board member, I used to say, "you may not get any pay, but at least you get a lot of grief." Anyone who cares enough about K-12 education to be willing to serve deserves our encouragement and thanks.

It is mathematically impossible to put all nine on the School Board and still have a board of seven members.

So how about, this year, we create the opportunity to benefit from all of them, with a "School Board Advisory Board"?

No matter who wins, there will be six who don't. There's no way their votes on board business could be counted legally. Only elected board members can vote. But their comments at board meetings, and revealing how they would have voted on items, could be a significant contribution to board discussions and outcomes. Whoever they may turn out to be, it seems a shame to lose their commitment, enthusiasm and obvious abilities following Tuesday – if they would be

willing to serve in that way.
    Just a thought.

Columns of Democracy

Chapter Three/Policy

Introduction

A "newspaper" is much more than newsprint, printer's ink and a Web site. The content alone ranges from comics to crossword puzzles and sports scores to shopping specials. The best papers are their community's driving force, the institution that serves all others, such as business, education and government. They provide the information necessary for what the Declaration of Independence itemized as our rights to "Life, Liberty and the pursuit of Happiness." One of my local papers, The Gazette, has as its mission statement, "To guide the community's deliberation of public issues, motivating people to get involved in the process and advocating for solutions." That is the goal of this chapter's columns: to encourage communities' civil conversations regarding "public policy."

"Never Happen Again" Is Not Enough
The Gazette, February 28, 2018, p. A6

Similar columns: Iowa City Press-Citizen, March 7, 2018, p. A7; and The Daily Iowan, March 19, 2018, p. 4

When I read Vanessa Miller's report that an audit revealed "unacceptable risks" in the University of Iowa's emergency preparedness (Feb. 18), I was reminded of a story my mother liked to tell.

A woman returned home to find a penciled note left by her new cleaning woman. It read: "I'm sorry, but I can't work in a home that keeps an alligator in the bathtub. I would have said something earlier, but I did not think the situation would arise."

Our school superintendent advised new school board members, "I don't like surprises."

There are surprises in life. Situations arise one could never have anticipated. That's true.

But most disasters and crises are predictable.

Every computer hard drive will crash someday. Mine did a couple of weeks ago. I make lots of stupid computer mistakes, but not this one, this time. I didn't have to say, "This must never happen again." I was able to say, "Thank goodness there's a backup on an external hard drive."

Railroad companies know that without "positive train control," their trains can jump the tracks or crash into other trains, and people can die. City officials know that without winter housing for the homeless some may die from the cold. University officials know the medical, mental and behavioral consequences of students' excessive alcohol consumption.

And federal and state legislators (along with Iowa's governor) know that, so long as they march in lockstep with the National Rifle Association, more schoolchildren will be shot.

For those paid big bucks to lead institutions – legislators, corporate CEOs, university presidents, school superintendents – responsibility for identifying and preventing potential disasters is part of their job description. We're not talking about the equivalent of unpredictable alligators in bathtubs. We're talking systemic failures, as the UI audit suggests.

Yes, we want to learn from mistakes, to do better next time. But that no longer can be the "get out of jail free" card for the legislators and executives who've failed to do their "Job One." OK, yes, tell us what you're going to do so we, and others, won't be going through this again.

But our real question for you is why, after 300 school shootings, did you so miserably fail at your job of anticipating the danger, and preventing it from happening this time?

Create a Caring Community
The Gazette, September 13, 2015, p. C3

What does it take to create a civil society, a sense of community, a preservation of culture?

Our Declaration of Independence asserts that every American is "endowed by their Creator with certain unalienable Rights, that among these are Life, Liberty and the pursuit of Happiness."

The World Bank reports 2.2 billion people try to subsist on less than $2.00 a day. Our Census Bureau says 45 million Americans (half are children) live below the poverty threshold.

Poverty, whether here or abroad, can put quite a crimp in one's life, liberty and happiness. Indeed, a Princeton study found you *can* buy additional happiness – up to an annual income of $75,000.

(Additional income adds little or nothing.)

But even in a capitalist (or our corporatist) country, true happiness – self-actualization, sense of self-worth, a sense of community – requires more than money.

We're aware of income inequality, the gap between us and the 1%. But what of the happiness gap?

Let's say roughly 30% of Americans confront challenges and conditions – in addition to finding too much month at the end of the money – that limit their sense of self-fulfillment.

Clearly, we provide them some government and volunteer assistance. Equally clearly, it's not enough. And when money's tight the support is cut. That is, in part, due to the political power of the "I've got mine, Jack," "Greed is good," "I built that" persuasion.

Adam Edelen, Kentucky's state auditor of public accounts, said "it is not Christian" to cut health coverage; "maybe this side of the aisle should put down the books of Ayn Rand and pick up the books of Matthew, Mark, Luke and John."

The Pope and many religious leaders agree. Others draw similar conclusions from basic ethics and morality.

That ought to be enough. Unfortunately, it's not. Little rationale beyond trickle-down is required to enact billionaires' tax breaks. Programs for the 30% have to prove their tax savings – or increased businesses' profits.

Fortunately, this proof is often available – even if it should not need to be. Most of Senator Bernie

Sanders' proposals are not only supported by 50-to-80% of America's voters, they have been adopted by most industrialized nations, and found to produce more wealth than they cost.

The 30% are not just homeless drug addicts. Some belong to highly skilled trades, or hold graduate degrees, like a Ph.D. who can't find a teaching position.

Some cities find the cost of housing for the homeless is less than the total costs of keeping them on the streets.

Mandatory minimum sentences for non-violent crimes cost taxpayers, impact families, and reduce inmates' education and potential productivity. Tuition-free college education built our nation's economy after World War II with the GI Bill, California and New York's later, and Germany's today. The cost of four years in prison would pay for four years in college. Drug courts are cheaper than prison.

The 30% includes those who can't afford desperately needed dental and medical care. And yet universal single-payer health care costs less and returns more than emergency room visits – or even health insurance.

Concerned about the economy? It's 70% driven with consumer spending. Minimum wage increases will be spent immediately. A full employment, federal government as employer of last resort policy would create substantial improvements to our communities, increase the skills and self-esteem of those now welfare-dependent, and give the economy a boost.

There are similar approaches to other challenges confronting the 30%. Persons of color who, regardless of socio-economic status, must daily deal with systemic racism. Single mothers earning minimum wage. Persons with physical or mental disabilities. College grads, burdened with debt. Those who've lost homes or farms. Those addicted to alcohol or tobacco. Residents of East Los Angeles, without cars, who spend hours on buses in order to provide services to those in West LA.

How do we create a sense of community? We focus first on "doing well by doing good" for the 30%. Then on the "middle class." And last on the top 1%. Our only problem has been that we have it backwards.

Building Consensus on Iowa City's Vision, Future
Iowa City Press-Citizen, June 30, 2015, p. A9

When it comes to building new structures and preserving the old, Iowa City needs a process that produces consensus.

Iowa City's downtown was laid out in 1839. Like Iowa's 99 counties, it was literally designed for a horse and buggy age. One hundred years later, even with automobiles, the downtown neither had nor needed parking garages or parking meters. Its department stores, hardware stores, five movie theaters, barber shops (for the weekly "shave and a haircut"), Sears, Montgomery Ward and others with farm supplies, served Johnson County's farmers on Saturdays and residents every day.

Today that function is served by the Coral Ridge

Mall, with more than 100 businesses and 5,000 free parking spaces. There's no way downtown Iowa City can regain its 20th century role in competition with that mall. And no way could it handle the crowds if it did.

For years I've advocated a vision for our downtown of a small, quaint, walkable, livable, residential center of history, entertainment and restaurants – along with the minimal number of banks, grocery stores and other businesses to sustain that residential population. That's something downtown could become.

And because it is a vision shared by Marc Moen and the City Council, it is what it is becoming.

That's not to say everyone agrees with every detail. There are disagreements about building design, height, and location; the balance between those living in half-million-dollar condos and minimum-wage residents in low-income housing; and the destruction of historic structures, such as the Civil War cottages. ("Three brick cottages, dating to the mid-1800s, stand in the 600 block of South Dubuque Street in what was once the city's rail district. The panel deemed the cottages historically significant at its meeting on Thursday [December 11, 2014]." Andy Davis, "Panel: Dubuque St. Cottages Are Historically Significant," Iowa City Press-Citizen, December 12, 2014.)

Then there's the taxpayer funding of private ventures with TIFs and other benefits – my major disagreement. See, http://tinyurl.com/pntu8gr. But even on that I agree with Moen, whom I also appreciate for his civic commitment, aesthetic creativity – and patience. As he said at the June 8 council meeting regarding the TIF decisions, "I know there's a lot of controversy about this. ... It's a political decision whether it's a good idea or not."

When a developer is invited to accept taxpayers' money, whether from Congress or a city council, she should no more be criticized for accepting a foolish TIF than when she takes an irrational, legal, federal tax deduction. If blame there be, it should be laid at the feet of the politicians.

Moen is right. It is a political decision.

But political decisions call for political process. Democracy has never been perfect; it's just the least worst of the alternatives. Lawrence Ferlinghetti wrote in 1958, "I am waiting for someone to really discover America." Now at 96, he's still waiting – and so are we.

Historically legitimate, traditional, public building projects, such as schools, libraries, court houses and jails, do have a democratic process. Governments can't build them unless voters approve the sale of bonds – bonds repaid with taxpayers' increased taxes.

Ironically, there is no similar democratic process to control government's use of taxpayers' money to fund for-profit, private building projects. It may be "a political decision," but there is no political democratic process for arriving at that decision. Listening to citizen complaints after the decision has been made is not a meaningful democratic process.

The historic preservation process is worse. Many cities receive economic as well as aesthetic value from historic preservation. In Iowa City, with enough developer pressure, the council simply overrules the best judgment of historic preservation groups, zoning boards and previous planning documents. Andy Davis, "2 remaining Civil War-era cottages on Dubuque St. torn down," Iowa City Press-Citizen, May 29, 2015.

Imagine if the council voted all the money necessary to preserve the homes and buildings we agree should be preserved, and the developers had to hold bake sales to add more floors to their high rises.

Maybe we need to vote. Maybe quality polling would be sufficient. What we must have is a better, more democratic process for evolving consensus regarding the Iowa City we want – and the "political decisions" about destruction of the old and building the new to get us there.

Design Communities to Support Communication, Interaction and Learning
The Gazette, February 7, 2016, p. C4

There were a lot of activists' movements during the 1960s and '70s – anti-war, pro-environment, the rights of women and African Americans, among others – each with its own first priority.

As a commissioner of the Federal Communications Commission during those years, the ways in which those movements were impacted by the role of the mainstream media, and the rules by which commercial media operated and was regulated, became very clear.

The media reform movement was born and grew

out of that awareness. As I put it at the time, "Whatever is your first priority, your second priority has to be media reform" – which ultimately contributed the book title, Your Second Priority (2008).

It was a new way of thinking about reform of government, politics, and public policy.

This year The Gazette intends to focus on our communities' opportunities, involving everything from affordable and integrated housing to health care, from parks and walkable cities to justice and police relations, economic growth to creative communities.

Just as activists can benefit by giving attention to the role of the media, so can those concerned about improving our communities benefit by considering the role of communications. Just as we have environmental impact statements, we might benefit from communications impact statements.

A 400-word column can't begin to identify the hundreds of categories of cities' communications opportunities, let alone explore them. But here are three illustrations.

Housing. Urban planning, the arrangement of suburban homes, or common space in apartment units, the availability of sidewalks and bike paths, can tend to increase, or decrease, chance meetings and conversation. Location of housing and schools can produce either the integration, or the segregation, of socio-economic classes, races and religions.

Analytics. The early Greeks spoke of analytics, and most city governments and residents have some access to data about their community and themselves. The movie "Money Ball" dramatized analytics' relevance to baseball. But the City of Boston has pushed it to a whole new level.

Learning communities. Learning can be everywhere – not just museums (Iowa Hall), places (Devonian Gorge), structures (Plum Grove; Mormon handcart site). It can also come from watching a sushi chef, or reading a business building's history on a plaque. There are thousands more words to be written about our communities' second priority. And we haven't even touched on more obvious features, such as public access cable channels, Web sites, blogs, meeting spaces, and libraries.

Think about it. We can do it.

Cancer: "Of Course; But Maybe"
The Gazette, July 17, 2016, p. 6A

Louis C.K. has a stand-up bit he calls, "Of Course...; but maybe. ..."

The White House's Cancer Moonshot Summit June 29 brought it to mind.

Vice President Joe Biden has been tasked with accomplishing ten years of cancer progress in the next five years.

Louis C.K. hasn't used "Of course...; but maybe..." regarding health care, but he could. Here's my example, based on UNICEF's reporting one billion people "don't have a safe water supply within fifteen minutes' walk" and "a lack of clean water and basic sanitation is responsible for 1.6 million preventable child deaths each year."

"Of course, we should develop more medicines to treat children's diseases from impure water. Of course. We should provide medicines and personnel to help those children. Of course, we should. But maybe, just maybe, we should also provide those children easy access to pure water and sanitation facilities."

The Cancer Moonshot program, and Vice President Biden's speech at the Summit, almost exclusively focus on the detection and treatment of the roughly 200 forms of cancer.

Most of the 20 "activities to support the goals of the Cancer Moonshot" involve drugs – easing and speeding their discovery, clinical trials, patents, and patients' access. There is genetic research, and the search for effective and less toxic therapies. Some programs are efforts to improve communication and coordination between agencies, institutions, researchers and doctors, the creation and sharing of big data and the Genomic Data Commons, and speeding up information distribution.

"Of course, we should launch a Cancer Moonshot, find a cancer cure, and alleviate patients' suffering from cancer and its treatment. Of course, we should support doctors' research. Of course. But maybe, just maybe, we should devote at least as much in the way of personnel and resources to discovering and eliminating the carcinogens to which we are all exposed."

When Washington Post reporters Bob Woodward and Carl Bernstein set out to understand and report the story of the 1972 Watergate break-in, one of their most useful sources was FBI Associate Director Mark Felt – known only as Deep Throat until he revealed his identity in 2005.

Never direct or fulsome, Deep Throat's suggestions sounded more like those in a Zen master's koan. One of his most useful was, simply, "Follow the money."

It's equally useful advice in our search for cancer's causes.

Who profits from cancer? Not who profits from researching and treating it. Who profits from causing cancer?

Major causes of cancer are carcinogens – substances in our homes, workplaces, air we breathe, water we drink, and food we eat.

The National Institute for Occupational Safety and Health lists 132 known carcinogens – just in the workplace. Physicians for Social Responsibility provides 10 categories of carcinogens and their cancers.

Virtually all carcinogens are the products or byproducts of corporations. In addition to which there are 100,000 additional substances we ingest that haven't even been tested – thanks to a subservient Congress.

The tobacco industry hooks junior high kids (the "replacement smokers" for the 400,000 it kills annually) on its cancer-causing product with addictive nicotine.

But most of our exposure to corporate cancer results from neither our choice nor a corporate executive's homicidal tendencies. It's the result of our unawareness, congressional subservience, and corporate executives' everyday profit maximization (ingredients with carcinogens may be cheaper than safer alternatives), apathy, or ignorance.

"Of course, we should support cancer research and treatment. But maybe, just maybe, we should also go after the corporations that are profiting from the carcinogens that cause the problem."

Recognizing and Reducing Racism
The Gazette, Gazette Writers Circle, August 9, 2015, p. C2

Text below [in brackets] was submitted to The Gazette but omitted from its hard copy and online editions.

I am about as familiar as an Iowa white boy can be with the evil consequences of racism as a result of spending most of the 1950s in Texas and throughout the South. Then there were still poll taxes designed to keep blacks from voting, black and white water fountains and restrooms, "No Colored" signs in restaurants' and stores' windows, and the need for a lawsuit to open a law school to blacks. Crosses were burned in the yards of the U.S. Court of Appeals judges with whom I worked in our efforts to right these wrongs.

Such experiences helped shaped my reaction as an F.C.C. commissioner upon discovering that the broadcasting industry the Commission was supposed to regulate "in the public interest" was one of, if not the country's most racist and sexist industries. I pushed for, and the Commission achieved, increased employment of African Americans and women in front of the cameras, broadcast management, and ownership.

But there is no comparison between being a compassionate observer and being an unwilling target in such a world.

Make no mistake. The offensive Confederate flags may be coming down, but racism is still with us [south, north, east and west. Today's blacks' lives are more likely to be threatened by a bullet from a gun than a rope from a tree, but their churches are still burned by a match from an arsonist.]

The Southern Poverty Law Center's annual measure of hate groups in the U.S. indicates that while the groups numbered from 131 to 149 during 2001 to 2008, during President Obama's presidency, from 2010 through 2014, the number ranged from 824 to 1360.

For those blacks able to avoid death, more common are the daily reminders of the painful ways in which they may have been negatively judged solely because of the color of their skin.

In one study, thousands of resumes were mailed to employers, identical except for the applicants' names. Black-sounding names were 50% less likely to be called back.

Black people are charged prices roughly $700 higher than white people when buying the same cars.

Multiple studies show black drivers are twice as likely to get pulled over for the same driving behavior.

Realtors will show black clients 18% fewer of the available homes than they show whites.

Although blacks and whites are roughly equal marijuana users, black people are four times more likely to be arrested.

Black people are incarcerated at nearly six times the rate of white people.

In another study, doctors did not inform black patients as often as white ones about an important heart procedure.

White legislators – from both major parties – did not respond as frequently to constituents with black sounding names as whites.

So what is meant by "white privilege"? It's what stand-up comic Louis C.K. is talking about when he says, "I've got a lot going for me: I'm healthy, I'm relatively young, I'm white. That is a huge leg up. Are you kidding me? I love being white. Let me be clear, by the way. I'm not saying that white people are better. I'm saying that being white is clearly better. Who could even argue?"

Harvard professor Mahzarin Banaji reports that even young black children absorb the social construct that white skin is prestigious and black skin isn't.

But to truly understand the consequences of the systemic racism in the lives of our African American friends and neighbors, we must do more than merely acknowledge its existence. We probably need to feel it emotionally before we will act.

[Here are some videos that may help: two TED talks, each watched over one million times, plus a powerful poet's presentation.

Start with James A. White's experience trying to find housing – http://tinyurl.com/oanhvnm.

Then watch and listen to the passion of poet Crystal Valentine's "On Evaluating 'Black Privilege'" –

https://www.youtube.com/watch?v=alh09OiwuA0.

Follow that with what diversity advocate Vernā Myers urges will make things better: http://tinyurl.com/pvltkob.

Then do your own search for the additional videos on the Internet providing an opportunity to know and enjoy the people and benefits of living in communities with rich racial, ethnic, religious, and cultural diversity.]

Health Care, Housing Rights?
The Gazette, August 1, 2017, p. A5

There's been discussion recently about housing (locally) and health care policy (nationally). Unlike government-funded programs used by all, these are programs for those most in need.

Developing public policy for social programs seems to be, as President Trump famously said, "an unbelievably complex subject. Nobody knew that [it] could be so complicated."

That's not precisely accurate. We are blessed with thousands of knowledgeable, caring individuals who do know how complicated it is.

Do you and I have (legally) or feel (morally) obligations to care for those beyond our family or community? To what extent do others have a "right" to expect such care?

Former Congressman Joe Walsh unambiguously put in his answer: "Health care is not a right. Housing is not a right. A job is not a right. College is not a right."

If health care is a product and housing is a privilege; if a majority believe and act as if the needy have no "rights" and we have no "obligations" that pretty much ends the discussion.

Where to find insight?

Religion? Jesus said, "Thou shalt love thy neighbor as thyself" and "Inasmuch as ye have done it unto one of the least of these my brethren, ye have done it unto me." The Bahai Universal House of Justice cites 16 major religions espousing the Golden Rule.

Founding documents? "We hold these truths to be self-evident, that all men are created equal, that they are endowed by their Creator with certain unalienable Rights, that among these are Life, Liberty and the pursuit of Happiness."

Virtually all the world's great religions, and nations agree we have some obligations to fellow members of our species. And yet, Walsh speaks for many Americans.

That's somewhere between ironic and inexplicable, given more U.S. citizens say "religion is very important in their lives" than people elsewhere. How can we square denying health care with caring for "the least of these"?

Could it be our "representatives" have adopted their major donors' belief that "my right to even bigger tax cuts trumps (so to speak) your right to come in out of the cold"?

Curbing Waste: Bad News, Good News
The Gazette, June 7, 2015, p. C1

"Wasted" can refer to our money, health, food, building materials, garbage, last year's fashions, lives of the most desperate of our fellow humans – or a binge drinking college student.

Does the built-in obsolescence of corporations' products or companies encouraging conspicuous consumption of "the latest thing" create "waste"?

Rudyard Kipling advised us to "fill the unforgiving minute/With sixty seconds' worth of distance run." Are minutes less filled a waste of time?

This column leaves those questions to others while focusing on next steps. Once there's agreement on what "waste" is, what can we do about it? How, if at all, can Americans be motivated to change?

Here are some illustrations.

Last month we celebrated "Bike to Work Week." Compared to car costs (running over 40 cents a mile), bicycling is virtually free. For short trips, with easier parking, they can be faster. They don't require drilling in the Artic wilderness, or military protection of "our oil" under others' sand. They don't pollute or accelerate climate change. Biking keeps you trim, happy and healthy, reducing your (and our nation's) health care costs.

One member of this Writers Circle walks, bikes, and seldom drives over 400 miles a year. The Sierra Club calculates that even far less – substituting a couple short bike rides for car trips each week – would save 2 billion gallons of gas, its impact on climate change, and billions of dollars.

Future wars will be fought over water. The best shower? Get wet. Turn off the water. Suds up. Rinse off. It's both more effective and efficient than running water for 20 minutes. If millions would do it, billions of gallons would be saved.

The same can be said for turning off the lights when you leave a room or throwing cans in a recycling basket rather than the wastebasket.

The literature is replete with hundreds more examples. We know what to do. And it takes little time or sacrifice to do it.

The problem? Americans don't have to be Libertarians to believe the Constitution guarantees their right to act in ways a majority considers stupid – so long as they don't harm others. As President Lyndon Johnson used to say, "I don't shove worth a damn." What we need is better understanding of how to motivate such people without criminalizing their behavior or denying them their choice.

But how?

Bad boys, for devilment, used to tie a tin can on a dog's tail and watch it try to outrun the noise. It gave rise to one Writers Circle member's insight: "tie your reform to the tail of greed, and watch it run off down the street." Otherwise put, "You get what you measure," or what you incentivize – whether the standards for faculty tenure, or manufacturers' installation of seat belts once they're mandated for the federal government's cars.

We can be motivated by education, information, appeals by celebrities – whether public service announcements, such as anti-smoking TV spots, or programming. When the Harvard School of Public Health asked Hollywood producers to include in their films shots of drivers fastening seat belts, lives were saved as public compliance followed.

Informed discussions among those chosen as scientific polling samples produce more thoughtful responses. What's called "deliberative democracy polling" could radically alter the public's and politicians' views on public policy.

The five-cent deposit on cans and bottles encourages recycling. Lower auto insurance rates for accident-free drivers encourages safer driving. "Cap and trade" pollution reduction (income for reduced pollution; with a choice to pay to pollute more) seems to work. A restaurateur's smoke-free restaurant (before legally required) actually attracted more customers.

Some major corporations are discovering it's profitable to move from a linear economy (raw materials to manufacturing, to sale and use, to landfill) to a circular economy (raw materials to manufacturing, to sale and use, to reuse of products' raw materials through restoration and resale). This not only reduces waste of non-renewable resources. Unilever's 240 factories in 67 countries now send zero waste to landfills. The sale of an electric car transportation service (rather than "a car"), for a monthly charge, with "new" rebuilt cars and batteries every three years, would be a win-win-win for manufacturers, dealers, drivers – and the planet.

No matter how we define "waste," the bad news is there's no groundswell of support to stop it, given the protests of those who profit from it. The good news is that we can be motivated to change.

Some Basic Facts About Water
The Gazette, February 29, 2016, p. A6

Water.

First, some basic facts.

Life began in water; human life still does. Our bodies are a mix of star stuff and water – in the same proportions as Earth's surface. We need replenishment of two to three quarts daily.

But 80% of our society's consumption is used in agriculture (one gallon for each almond). More goes to industry, like fracking.

We each use about 100 gallons daily. For all Iowans that's 110 billion gallons annually.

Residents of Flint are right to worry about lead. Thousands of other cities ought to – 40% of reporting states have more lead poisoning than Flint. And the 15 parts per billion standard is not science based. It's chosen as a standard 90% of cities can pass.

But wait; it's worse. I used to hike where pure water came from springs and ran in streams. Today those sources can contain many of the 100,000 potentially toxic substances that have never been researched, tested, or regulated. Even if they were, one-third of Americans' water sources aren't covered by clean water laws.

Rain brings air pollutants, runoff brings fertilizer, industrial waste may be dumped, and nitrate removal treatments can leave toxic nitrosamines. More dangerous elements (like Flint's lead) can come from aging water mains, or pipes from the mains to, and inside, the home.

One of the greatest single "medical" advances for 2.5 billion of the world's people? Not a new AIDS or malaria drug. It would be pure drinking water and sanitary facilities for the two million who die every year without them.

There are other ways water can sicken or kill you. Worldwide, an estimated 372,000 people annually die from drowning – the third leading cause of unintentional injury death.

Ocean levels are rising at increasing rates, as warmer water expands and glaciers melt. If all land ice melted, oceans would rise 197 feet. That's not happening. But a possible 20-foot rise by 2100 would necessitate relocating a billion people.

And all that's the good news. Most serious? The coming severe water shortages and inevitable water wars.

Kind of puts our Iowa legislative proposals into perspective, doesn't it?

My proposals?

1. Prepare to spend $1 trillion on the infrastructure our grandparents built and we, preferring tax cuts, have allowed to rot.

2. Fund the scientific and medical research necessary to understand the human impact of all the substances in water, and then set standards.

3. Give Americans free access to test data about what comes out of their own faucets (not just what

comes out of their cities' treatment plants).

4. Finally, elect public officials who care more about our health than their donors' wealth.

Working Our Way Through the McGinness Kerfluffle
Iowa City Press-Citizen, September 20, 2013, p. A7

A Frenchman, asked why he kissed women on the hand, replied, "Because you have to start somewhere."

But where should one start with the porcupine of prickly issues emerging from the kerfluffle surrounding Jeff McGinness' difficulties? There's little about it you'd ever want to kiss anywhere.

In law professor fashion, I'm not offering answers – just questions. McGinness, school board members, citizens, the Press-Citizen – all of us need to think this through for ourselves.

But I do see some issues.

How should we go about judging what is, and is not, forgivable in others? Are there any normative principles? Or is every case a one-off?

We can start with Iago's observation, "he that filches from me my good name Robs me of that which not enriches him And makes me poor indeed." Othello, Act 3, Scene 3.

Reputation is a valuable possession. Corporations put a dollar value on goodwill. Spreading

Policy – 101

falsehoods is defamation. The unnecessary spread of truth can also be harmful. At a minimum, we should think twice before speaking ill of others.

Deserved or not, the publicizing of one's faults is itself a serious punishment.

The forms of expressing disapproval extend over quite a range. It can take the form of a private thought, a whispered comment, public speech, or newspaper editorial. It can include a demand for resignation, or other punishment.

Suppose the irrefutable facts were that Governor Branstad regularly instructed his drivers to speed. (His Lt. Governor said they have a tight schedule – reminiscent of President Nixon's explanation to David Frost that, "When the President does it, that means it is not illegal.")

Would it be reasonable, or fair, to try to bring about his removal from office for this behavior? If he also served on a church's board of trustees, should he be asked to resign?

Does disapproved behavior at work warrant harsher penalties than if done in a bar, or at home?

Is it less bad if no one has suffered any physical, financial or reputational harm – aside from the perpetrator?

Should we distinguish between a weekend problem drinker who's a top employee, and one who shows up drunk, or drinks at work?

How serious would you consider a coach who covers up a valued player's crimes? A businessperson who lies about their "need" for a TIF? A professor who raises the failing grade of an athlete to keep him eligible? The university's administrator who requested she do so? Someone who files taxes late, and predates the check? A church official who moves a pedophile minister to another church? A negligent doctor, threatened with a malpractice suit, who forces his nurse to lie? An administrator who is known to be condescending and mean to store clerks, waiters, and trades persons working on his property?

Should these facts, if sufficiently proven, disqualify those persons from serving on the board of a local, non-profit, volunteer organization?

Does it make a difference whether a financial vice president embezzles funds from her company, or as treasurer of her church? What if she had an off-duty ethical lapse wholly unrelated to the kind of work she does? In short, does it make a difference that the wrongdoing involves a personal quality required by her job? That it was done elsewhere?

How far can one indiscretion fairly be stretched to general conclusions about character? During a trial, unless a party or witness raises character issues, there are limits on the introduction of past derelictions. Of course, in our day-to-day lives we have neither the resources nor the restraints of trial lawyers. One lie may not legitimately make one "a liar." But we recall "fool me once, shame on you; fool me twice, shame on me."

Finally, we're voters. We can vote for or against elected officials for whatever fool reasons we want. But we'll feel better about ourselves if we've been thoughtful and fair in our judgments.

Chapter Four/Politics

Introduction

Politics is process, the process that uses the columns of democracy – including our constitutionally protected freedom of speech, assembly and right to petition the government – to redress grievances and transform policy into law. Unfortunately, few politicians share the view, once told me by Joe Biden, that "there are some things worth losing an election for." Too many politicians believe, like football coaches Vince Lombardi and Red Saunders, that "winning isn't everything, it's the only thing." Anything they can get away with that will tilt the playing field their direction is acceptable – massive campaign spending, requiring voter identification, purging the registration rolls, or redrawing a state's legislative and congressional districts ("gerrymandering"). But this chapter, like the others, is not an integrated essay on the blessings and burdens of politics. It's merely a collection of columns published during 2013-2017 that are in some way related to politics. Three urge support for individual candidates. "Believing is Seeing" addresses the biology of impenetrable ideology. Two contain early thoughts regarding Trump. And one analyzes the Republicans' reliance on "the peoples' voice" to justify their refusal to hold hearings on President Barack Obama's nomination of Merrick Garland to the Supreme Court.

When Believing Is Seeing
Iowa City Press-Citizen, July 14, 2014, p. A5

Hitler's Joseph Goebbels is credited with the strategy that, "If you repeat a lie often enough, people will believe it." That's deliberate lying.

More common is Mark Twain's insight that, "It's not what we don't know that's the problem, it's what we know that ain't so." We're not "lying." We're just repeating false information we assume is true because it's consistent with our beliefs – something journalists are trained to guard against.

New York's four-term U.S. Senator Daniel Moynihan famously admonished, "Everyone is entitled to his own opinion, but not to his own facts."

But what are we to do when it is our opinion that creates our facts?

"Seeing is believing?" Yes, sometimes. But the reverse is also true: "Believing is seeing." We tend to see that which supports our beliefs.

In a Yale paper last year, "Motivated Numeracy and Enlightened Self-Government," the authors report their research finding that even scientists, highly skilled in math, make more errors when the correct math answer leads to conclusions contrary to their political orientation.

The phenomenon occurs for what we love as well as what we hate. Fans of Pope Francis are likely to believe favorable, false stories about his good deeds, however implausible (*e.g.*, he's slipping out at night to visit Rome's homeless). See, "Snopes, Popes and Presidents," http://bit.ly/1mRLzLY.

Similarly, Obama haters are equally willing to believe almost any emailed negative assertion about our "Muslim, socialist, Kenyan, imperial" president – and send it on.

Snopes.com is a wonderful online service for checking the truth of the "urban legends, folklore, myths, rumors, and misinformation" that circle the global Internet each day. When the occasional Obama-haters' email comes our way, we check it on Snopes.com, and kindly inform the senders if the email is untrue.

Recently came a whopper, widely circulated since January.

It was so obviously wrong on so many counts it would have been hilarious if it hadn't been seriously libelous in its efforts to link the President – and Hillary Clinton, too, for good measure – to words allegedly authored by community organizer Saul Alinsky: "Eight steps required to create a socialist state."

To paraphrase Senator Lloyd Bentsen's retort when Senator Dan Quayle compared himself to President Jack Kennedy during their 1988 vice presidential candidate debate, "I knew Saul Alinsky. Saul Alinsky was a friend of mine. And believe me, Sir, Saul Alinsky never wrote those words."

Nor could Barack Obama have received the mentoring from Alinsky the email hints at, since President Obama was only 10 years old when Alinsky died. In fact, during a conversation I once had with candidate Obama about community organizing, neither of us even mentioned Alinsky's name.

The need to oppose and demonstrate the evil in

everything President Obama has ever read, thought, advocated or done can lead to bizarre results, one of which is the email's effort to demonize community organizing as "socialism." It not only reveals equal ignorance regarding both but rejects what is just another description of democracy.

Community organizing is the study, design, and utilization of strategies by which neighborhoods, or other groups of individual citizens, can more effectively present their grievances and proposals to governments and other institutions. These are techniques millions have proudly used since our nation's birth, including both the Tea Party and Occupy movements during this century.

What can we do?

MSNBC's Rachel Maddow simply tries to state the facts occasionally. Examples: "He really was born in Hawaii. And climate change is real. And rape really does cause pregnancy sometimes. And evolution is a thing. And no one is taking away anyone's guns. And the moon landing was real. And regulations of the financial services industry are not the same thing as communism."

You get the idea.

And for the rest of us? "Check it on Snopes or risk looking like dopes."

Senate Ignoring the People's Voice
Iowa City Press-Citizen, April 8, 2016, p. A5

Also as: Iowa City Press-Citizen Online, April 7, 2016; Des Moines Register Online, April 8, 2016; "Examining the 'People's Voice,'" The Gazette, April 10, 2016, p. A3, The Gazette (online), April 10, 2016; "The Constitution, Supreme Court, and People's Voice," The Daily Iowan, April 15, 2016, p. 4.

The U.S. Constitution mandates that the President "shall nominate, and by and with the Advice and Consent of the Senate, shall appoint...Judges of the supreme Court ...." [Art. 2, Sec. 2.]

Following the death of Justice Antonin Scalia on Feb. 13, President Obama sent the Senate his nomination of Judge Merrick Garland.

Of course, any senator can vote "no" on Garland's confirmation.

That's not enough for today's Republican Senate leadership. It totally rejects all portions of the confirmation process.

In 1987, President Ronald Reagan nominated Judge Robert Bork for the Supreme Court. Bork's Senate hearing went badly. Nonetheless, his commitment to the Constitution caused him to insist on the full Senate's confirmation debate and vote he knew he'd lose, saying "A crucial principle is at stake...the deliberative process."

Given that the Republican Party professes as much allegiance to a literal reading of the Constitution as of the Bible, their Senate leaders' refusal to vote is difficult to square with either the language of the Constitution or its interpretation by their poster judge, Robert Bork.

What justification do they offer? Majority Leader Mitch McConnell says they want to "give the people a voice" in the selection of Supreme Court justices. Let's examine this rationale.

1. For starters, the Constitution's drafters were more interested in muffling the people's voice than in sharing the establishment's power with "the people."

2. Ours was not to be a direct democracy with decisions made by national referenda. Elected representatives would make the decisions.

3. There were severe restrictions on who could vote – initially only land-owning, white males over 21. African-Americans got the vote in 1870 (15th Amendment), women in 1920 (Amendment 19), and 18-20-year-olds in 1971 (Amendment 26).

4. The drafters restricted for whom citizens could vote. Still today, we won't be voting for president next November. The Constitution says our president will be selected, not by the people's voice or vote, but by "electors" appointed by each "State...in such Manner as the Legislature thereof may direct." (Art. 2, Sec. 1.)

5. Nor could "the people" even select U.S. senators. "The Senate...shall be ... of two Senators from each State, chosen by the Legislature thereof." (Art. 1, Sec. 3; changed in 1913, Amendment 17.)

6. Thus, respect for Justice Scalia's search for "original meaning" should preclude Senators Mitch McConnell's and Charles Grassley's deference to a "people's voice" in the judicial confirmation process.

7. Even if constitutionally relevant, which it's not, that people's voice was clearly heard with the election of President Obama in 2008 and 2012. And the Constitution offers no hint that a president's judicial appointment power is any less on the last day of his or

her presidency than on the first.

8. If the popular vote in presidential elections is "the people's voice," what is it saying? At best, a majority's preference between two candidates.

9. Although not constitutionally compelling, theoretically a presidential campaign could turn on one single, dominant issue. But that wasn't true in 2008 or 2012. Clearly, neither of those elections raised, let alone resolved, the Senate's constitutional right to refuse to undertake confirmation proceedings.

10. These points are equally applicable to Senator McConnell's insistence that the 2014 election of Republican senators was a people's voice for Senate refusal to hold judicial confirmation proceedings.

The Constitution's drafters knew the court's justices could only function as intended if the public believed they were independent and non-partisan, able, honest and just.

The Republican Senate leadership's response to Judge Garland is wrong, both constitutionally and in their "people's voice" rationale. It also further erodes public confidence in our unique and precious judicial institutions.

Whether they are also wrong that their chosen path will best serve their political self-interest we will only know after the people's voice is unambiguously heard in next November's Senate elections.

Trump Might Not Be Blundering in Race
Iowa City Press-Citizen, September 9, 2016, p. A7

Donald Trump says we don't understand him. "These politicians, they don't know me. They don't understand me." He's right. Politicians, reporters and voters have had little to go on beyond speculation about his motives.

Some armchair psychiatrists think he displays evidence of classic narcissism. Others believe he's just naturally mean-spirited and crude when he disparages captured military personnel, women, people with disabilities, Muslims, Gold Star families – whoever's in view when his mouth opens.

There's speculation he's never been serious about running, surprised he won the nomination, and is already preparing for a loss – blaming a hostile media ("the lowest form of life") and "rigged" voting.

But wait; there's more.

There are at least three ways to get the goods and services for a political campaign: pay for them yourself, solicit and spend others' campaign contributions, or get what you need without paying.

Given the proportion of campaign advertising dollars spent on radio and TV (80 percent) getting it free is the preferred option.

So how has Donald Trump made out with free media? Like a bandit! Two billion dollars' worth by March this year.

Which brings us to a possible understanding of Trump.

One of his wildest and most recent assertions is that ISIS was created by President Barack Obama, its "founder."

Many, including myself, have noted that our entry into Iraq, exit, and then re-entry have increased recruitment of terrorists and attacks on American military. When Trump appeared on conservative talk radio host Hugh Hewitt's program, Hewitt tried to use this analysis to help Trump. Trump was having none of it:

Hugh Hewitt: You said the President was the founder of ISIS. I know what you meant. You meant that he created the vacuum, he lost the peace.

Donald Trump: No, I meant he's the founder of ISIS.

HH: But he's not sympathetic to them. He hates them. He's trying to kill them.

DT: I don't care. He was the founder.

HH: But by using the term "founder," they're hitting you on this again. Mistake?

DT: No, it's no mistake. Everyone's liking it. Do you not like that?

HH: I don't. I think I would say they created the vacuum into which ISIS came, but they didn't create ISIS. That's what I would say . . . I'd just use different language to communicate it.

DT: But they wouldn't talk about your language, and they do talk about my language, right?

HH: Well, good point.

"They do talk about my language." Trump's six

words tell the tale. Maybe Trump's strategy is that there's no bad publicity – especially when it's a $2 billion value for free.

And recall his brag Fortune reported, "I could be the first presidential candidate to run and make money on it." Already roughly 20 percent of his campaign expenditures involve payments to his own companies.

Plus, since much of his "property" is his brand, his name, he will continue to make money post-election – not to mention larger royalties for ghost-written books, lecture fees and a higher rated TV show.

His is a win-win strategy. If his loyal followers deliver 270 electoral votes, he's president. If not, the value of his brand, his name on his properties, will have increased by hundreds of millions, if not billions, of dollars.

And all because, as he says, "they do talk about my language, right?"

Republicans Need to Get Their Party Back From Trump
Iowa City Press-Citizen, October 20, 2016, p. 7A

Iowa's statewide and congressional elected officials – Gov. Terry Branstad, U.S. Sens. Chuck Grassley and Joni Ernst, and U.S. Reps. Rod Blum, David Young, and Steve King – are doing great harm to Iowa, themselves and a future Republican Party by continuing their endorsements of Donald Trump.

This is not a partisan, pro-Hillary Clinton judgment. I supported Sen. Bernie Sanders.

As a Democrat, I want to "make the Republican Party great again." The evolution of a democracy's wise public policy requires the thorough consideration of alternatives that can only emerge from civil, cooperative – and yes, compromising – conversation between those whose differing opinions are grounded in agreed-upon facts.

I'm old enough to remember that Republican Party, and to long for its return. That day is only delayed by Republican officials who say, in effect, that Donald Trump's actions and words represent their values.

Is Donald Trump really someone they hold up to their children as a model? Do they really think he has the knowledge of domestic needs and world affairs, experience in government, mature judgment, people skills, respect for others and the values to be one of America's best presidents? Is he even a conservative?

Numerous Republican officials share my view.

The party's highest ranked official (Speaker Paul Ryan), most recent presidents (George H.W. Bush and George W. Bush), and presidential candidates (Sen. John McCain and former Massachusetts Gov. Mitt Romney) have refused to support Trump.

Now, they've been joined by over 50 leading Republicans – governors, U.S. senators and representatives – who either never did, or do not now, support him. Some think Trump should drop out. Some say they'll vote for Hillary Clinton. Others merely say they can't endorse or vote for him.

By early October, no major U.S. newspaper had

endorsed Trump. Some conservative papers that have never endorsed a Democrat are supporting Hillary Clinton; others merely advise readers not to vote for Trump.

One can sympathize with Iowa's Republican leaders. It's not easy to reject one's presidential nominee. But the cost of their supporting Trump far exceeds any benefit.

1. That they supported Trump will forever be a large blot on their personal political legacy.

2. It will make it more difficult to rebuild a new, improved, responsible Republican Party in Iowa and the U.S., especially while Trump attacks Republican leaders.

3. Trump's stirring up even more divisiveness and polarization is a disservice. It brings out the worst in us, rather than our best. Iowa's leaders are encouraging emulation of someone who deals in ridicule and mean-spirited disparagement of women, entire races, religions, ethnicities; war heroes, people with disabilities and Gold Star mothers.

4. Iowans are proud of their reputation for "Iowa nice," their welcoming of immigrant populations from around the world, their ethical and religious values – a culture diametrically opposed to what Trump represents.

5. Iowans, like all Americans, want our state to be well thought of by others – especially those with ill-informed biases who think we're just backwater, flyover country. Our leaders' support for Trump only reinforces our critics' worst prejudices.

6. We are trying to attract the best and the

brightest to our state – faculty and students, leaders of large and small businesses, skilled workers and the creative class. We want to retain our first-in-the-nation presidential caucuses. Other states have lost business for being far less offensive than Trump.

Iowa's Republican officials don't need to drop their membership in the Republican Party, or announce they are voting for Hillary Clinton. They don't need to publicly itemize the daily lengthening list of reasons why Trump is unsuited to be president.

What they do need to do, for their own sake and that of their constituents, is to join the impressive ranks of responsible Republicans who have announced they are neither endorsing nor voting for Donald Trump.

Sanders the Right Democrat for Caucus
Iowa City Press-Citizen, January 22, 2016, p. A7

Also as: Sanders the Right Democrat for Caucus, Iowa City Press-Citizen (online), January 21, 2016; Why I'm Caucusing for Sanders, The Gazette, January 26, 2016, p. A8, Why I'm Supporting Bernie Sanders for President," The Gazette (online), January 26, 2016; and Why Support Sanders, The Daily Iowan, January 28, 2016, p. A4

This is the story of how I came to support Sen. Bernie Sanders. It's a true story – or at least as true as a fading memory can provide.

Some 40 years ago in Washington, I agreed to

host a series of TV interviews with presidential candidates. Questioning the first few proved problematic. Their responses to questions seemed to be coming from tape cassettes implanted in their skulls. They'd heard the questions before, and we'd heard their answers.

How to make their performances more revealing? The possibilities of someone tipping over a candidate's chair, or unexpectedly throwing them a baseball, were attractive but rejected by the producer.

The ultimate solution was found in a question put to presidential candidates then, and throughout the years since, often in Iowa living rooms. "Senator, let's make two assumptions. One, those of us here think you are 'right on the issues.' And two, you are elected president. Now tell us, why will coal mine owners have less ability to maintain coal miners' unsafe working conditions than they do now?" One could substitute the military-industrial complex's control of defense budgets, or oil company subsidies.

Some candidates would stare blankly. Some would become angry. Apparently, few if any had ever thought about the problem, and none offered a solution.

When I put the question to Sen. Barack Obama in 2007, he replied, "Well, Nick, I've been a community organizer." I'd visited with Saul Alinsky and read his books. Both Obama and I were familiar with Heather Booth's Midwest Academy in Chicago, where I'd learned community organizing. I too quickly leapt to the conclusion that Obama got it. He would become our national community organizer-in-chief! I was mistaken.

Sen. Sanders not only gets it, he makes it explicit.

He rejects chants of "Bernie, Bernie" with "this is not about 'me,' it's about 'we.'" "This campaign is about creating a movement of millions of Americans fighting to transform our country with demands that government represent all of us," he's said.

Of course, like most Americans, I like his specific proposals – increased minimum wage, health care for all, higher taxes on the wealthy, avoiding unnecessary wars, tuition-free college, jobs improving infrastructure and many more.

But far more important than the specifics is his belief that government should serve all the people, the socioeconomic bottom 50 percent as well as the top 1 percent. That a government of the major donors, by the lobbyists, for the wealthy is not what the founders had in mind. That when candidates of either the Democratic or Republican parties' establishment talk of proposals, the results look a lot more like capitulation in the cause of campaign contributions than compromise on behalf of the American people.

Of course, I'm impressed with the more conventional things said about Sen. Sanders. His authenticity. His enormous, enthusiastic crowds, and millions of supporters. That he not only talks against Wall Street and PAC funding, he walks the walk by refusing their money, while raising enough from small donors. He's had experience as a mayor, congressman and senator, one who understands the federal government's working and impact. Up against Republican candidates, he's as electable as other Democrats. He has the best "favorability" numbers.

But most important to me? His lifelong advocacy

that governments exist for the 99 percent. His ability to answer my 40-year-old question; his knowledge of what's required for a government to serve the people. A campaign that's already begun building that citizen organization.

Are you in the 1 percent? There are establishment candidates for you. If not, whether Republican, Democrat, Libertarian or Green, it serves your interest and mine if Sen. Sanders' vision and voice come booming out of Iowa's precinct caucuses, loud and clear across America throughout 2016. It's up to you.

Throgmorton Is City Treasure
Iowa City Press-Citizen, October 28, 2015, p. A13

Jim Throgmorton is a real Iowa City treasure as a City Council member, someone we ought to encourage to keep at it as long as he can stand this often-thankless job.

He holds a Ph.D. in urban and regional planning from UCLA. He taught the subject for 24 years as a professor at the University of Iowa. He contributes to and keeps up with the literature and is knowledgeable regarding cities' "best practices." He has had two tours of duty with the Iowa City Council (1993-95; 2011-present) and is otherwise embedded in our community and culture. In addition to Iowa City and Los Angeles, he is familiar with Chicago, Kansas City, Louisville, and many other cities in this country and Germany.

Unlike his opponents, and those who stole our yard sign, Jim believes all Iowa City residents deserve to be heard – including Iowa City's 1%, developers, and business owners. But he also knows the best policies emerge when officials' views are tested and challenged – including his own.

To let the 1% remove him from the council would no more serve their own selfish interests – let alone the rest of us – than when we let the Regents run David Skorton out of town.

Re-elect Rettig for Supe, She Knows What She's Doing
Iowa CityPress-Citizen, May 17, 2014
With Mary Vasey.

Janelle Rettig is worthy of your vote for Johnson County Supervisor on or before June 3.

In our lifetimes of dealing with politicians and officials at the local, county, state and federal governmental level in this country and abroad, she stands out as one of the best.

Rettig has our vote and support because she knows what she's doing, works hard, does her research, listens, answers questions and concerns, and finds satisfaction in serving everyone in Johnson County.

She also happens to be a wonderful person. We could go on and on about Rettig and her joy in living, but it embarrasses her. So we'll stop now.

Just don't forget to vote for Rettig for Supervisor on June 3.

Chapter Five/Taxes

Introduction

During 2013-2017 there were enough columns regarding taxation to earn their own chapter. What are we trying to accomplish with tax policy? What are the impacts of sales taxes and gasoline taxes on income inequality?

There were a disproportionate number of columns about TIFs – taxpayers' funding developers. They come next. Finally, there are a group of columns dealing with taxation for legitimate public projects – in this case bonds for a county courthouse expansion.

Decisions Must Come Before Taxes
The Gazette, January 3, 2018, p. A5

Also: Taxes Are Last Step, Not the First, to Making U.S. Great, Iowa City Press-Citizen, January 27, 2018, p. A6

  The worst thing about tax cut discussions is the "Oh, look at the squirrel" distraction from what we should be talking about.
  Example? Cutting Iowa employers' taxes can't create more jobs when employers say their real problem is a shortage of skilled workers.
  If a skilled workforce is needed, it's time to increase, not slash, funding for the state's universities

and community colleges that create those workers.

What is your vision for America?

Some believe we are a nation of 320 million rugged individualists, where everyone is obliged to pull themselves up by their own bootstraps – even those without boots. As Grover Norquist revealed, "My goal is to get government down to the size where we can drown it in the bathtub."

Others believe those benefiting from a community are morally obliged to care for everyone in the human family. Some cite Jesus' urging us to provide food, drink, clothing, health care, and prison visits for "the least of these."

Until we decide whether we want an America of rugged individualism or humanitarianism, little agreement on public policy can follow.

This newspaper is full of reporting and opinion about our plethora of policy challenges – affordable housing, education, environment, flood control, health care, homelessness, hunger, jobs, net neutrality, refugees, transportation, water quality. The Gazette's Iowa Ideas project explores some answers.

Lynda Waddington recently described Philip Alston's U.N. report on U.S. poverty and human rights. Read his comparative rankings for U.S. infant mortality (highest), water and sanitation (36th in the world), incarceration rate (highest), youth poverty (highest), poverty and inequality (35th of 37). [Philip Alston, "Statement on Visit to the USA on Extreme Poverty and Human Rights," United Nations, Office of the High Commissioner Human Rights, December 15, 2017.]

We built this America. Is it the nation and state

you want? No? Then fix it. How do we do that? In order:
1. Don't start with tax talk.
2. Decide whether we're rugged individualists or humanitarians.
3. Provide enforcement of metrics for the values and society we want – for ourselves and "the least of these" – not just aspirations.
4. Develop public policies that can reach those goals.
5. Calculate their costs.
6. Explore ways of accomplishing goals through education and training, philanthropy and volunteerism, churches and trade unions, corporate policies and cost avoidance, other innovative approaches.
7. Propose a tax code, consistent with community values, sufficient to provide the remaining, necessary public funding. And remember:
(a) No tax cuts until there are surpluses and declining debt.
(b) When corporations and the wealthy have trillions of dollars they don't use, don't hand them more.
(c) Consumer spending drives 70 percent of the economy. If stimulus is needed, give the money to the bottom 80 percent who will spend it.
8. Vote.

Philip Alston reports that only 64 percent of Americans bother to register, and many of them don't vote. In Canada and the U.K., 91 percent register, 96 percent in Sweden, nearly 99 percent in Japan.

Could that possibly be a part of our problem?

Congress' First Step in Long Journey
The Gazette, April 4, 2013, p. A5

Democrats and Republicans in Washington are seemingly suffering from ideological immobilization regarding the national debt.

Republicans' Grover Norquist famously said he'd like a government small enough that he "can drown it in the bathtub."

Republicans fear that if taxes are increased, the liberal tax-and-spend Democrats will just squander the money on bigger government and more wasteful giveaways. Meanwhile, Democrats fear that free-range, feral Republicans will ultimately leave us with no solution for our surfeit of poor children other than Jonathan Swift's suggestion that we eat them.

I understand their dilemma. Being honorable men and women, they know that when you take hundreds of thousands of dollars from someone you have a moral obligation to reciprocate, to meet your donor's expectations of reward.

Years ago, I documented their expectations. The average rate of return was 1,000-to-one or more. The official gets a $100,000 "contribution"; the donor's repaid $100 million for his "investment." The payback can take the form of, say, subsidies, price supports, tax breaks, government contracts, public land, bailouts or tariffs.

The total isn't chump change. The International Monetary Fund says global subsidies for fossil fuels alone are $1.9 trillion a year.

Recently, 10 percent of the Fortune 500

corporations had so many tax breaks they not only owed no taxes, they received refund checks!

Sen. Tom Coburn, R-Oklahoma, explains what others fear to whisper: "It's not about tax policy, it's about benefiting the political class and the well-connected and the well-heeled in this country."

Legislators need money to be re-elected. Can you see why it's easier for them to cut Social Security or food stamps than their donors' rewards programs? (The poor are notoriously miserly when it comes to large campaign contributions.)

So, what's our nation's first step on this journey of a thousand miles?

Here's an idea. Ask the Congressional Budget Office and IRS to, first, identify all the special interest tax breaks that lobbyists have obtained. Some benefit an individual company, others an industry or all business. Forget the other trillions in giveaways; focus on tax breaks.

Don't eliminate these tax breaks; just make them visible subsidies, as appropriations. Publish them online. Hold news conferences to brief journalists and bloggers and let them run with it.

Then see what happens. If the public doesn't respond, well, that's democracy for you. If they do, it might provide some backbone implants for our "representatives" in Washington.

And Des Moines.

The Gazette's Erin Jordan has skillfully brought this approach to Iowa's sales tax. (March 23) "Report: Iowa lost $3.9 billion in sales tax breaks in 2010; Breaks up 62 percent since 2005."

I've written about applying it to TIFs (tax increment financing) – the local form of handing taxpayers' money over to for-profit businesses, as in "TIF Towers," http://fromdc2iowa.blogspot.com/2012/04/tif-towers.html.

When it comes to federal, state and local politicians transferring taxpayers' money to for-profit companies (often in exchange for campaign contributions), the practices and consequences are similar, whether the special treatment comes from local TIFs, state sales taxes or federal corporate income taxes.

The first step to reform is also similar: public disclosure of what's going on.

How much money is at stake? Who's getting it? In exchange for how much in campaign contributions?

Neither the media nor public in our democratic society can begin to redress these abuses so long as they take the form of essentially invisible tax breaks. These giveaways should be debated as appropriations openly arrived at and shamelessly set upon the table under lights.

If only Congress' journey of a thousand miles could begin with this simple, single step.

On the Local Option Sales Tax, Think Before You Vote

Iowa City Press-Citizen, October 8, 2014, p. A11

My response to the dueling sales tax columns on the Oct. 6 opinion page? Think before you vote. That's all I ask.

Income inequality is as American as apple pie. The wealthy get the largest slices. So it has always been.

The 18th Century sentiment, "Those who own the country ought to govern it," is attributed to John Jay, our first Supreme Court Chief Justice. It didn't just burst forth as a talking point from today's conservative rightwing corporatists or Fox News.

We're familiar with the results from Washington. One family owns more than do 40 percent of the American people combined. The increased value since the 2008 bank fraud has gone to the upper one percent – including those very bankers too big to jail.

What we and the media lose with our focus on Washington is that the same forces are playing out in state capitals, county courthouses, and city councils.

It would be hilarious if it was not so inhumane.

Why does the City Council tell us we need this sales tax increase? To make up for lowered property tax receipts, they say. And what are they going to do with the additional sales tax receipts? Why, use at least 40 percent of them to lower property taxes even further.

Read that a second time before you go on. Can you imagine what Jon Stewart would do with that one?

Landlords' apartments that the occupants don't own will now be taxed as if they did, with lower taxes for landlords. Guess how those savings will be divided between reductions in rents and increases in landlords' profits.

The rich become ever-richer because the tax laws are rigged. The wealthy have lower rates on profits from investing money than the working poor have on pay for investing physical effort.

Those who have to spend every dime they earn are the ones hit hardest by the sales tax. (That's why the quickest way out of the recession in our 70-percent consumer-spending economy would have been to flow money through their hands rather than the wealthy.)

Don't be fooled by this increase of "a penny," or "one percent." For the math-impaired, an increase from six percent to seven percent is closer to a 17 percent increase.

Be aware we are playing Washington's game right here in Iowa City. The Council is offering you a deliberate scheme to shift even more money from Iowa City's working poor to its upper middle class and rich. Washington's conservative corporatists would be proud.

You see, this is not just tax breaks for the rich – which it also is. It's worse. It's Robin Hood in reverse: further enriching our local well-off by taking money out of the pockets of those most in need.

Before you vote to take 17 percent more from those suffering the most, consult your head, your heart, your conscience, your God. Is that who you are? Is that who you really want to be?

Think Long and Hard Before Diluting the Gasoline Tax
Iowa City Press-Citizen, December 5, 2013, p. A7

As children, we used to sing "London Bridge Is Falling Down." That was fantasy. We'd never heard of a bridge falling down.

Now we have.

Why won't Gov. Branstad advocate an increase in the gasoline tax?

No one questions the need for safe, smooth roads and bridges.

Few question public ownership and maintenance. It sure beats private ownership by profit-maximizing corporations.

The only remaining issue? How to pay for it? As an earlier [Dec. 2] Press-Citizen editorial explained, the gasoline tax wins that one hands down.

We'll either pay for roads and bridges or we won't have them. But for a gasoline tax to pick up the tab, it must take account of inflation and current needs.

Politicians who run and vote against "government," encourage the notion taxes are evil. Taxes are just another way to buy stuff we need – like roads. Taxes are often the most efficient and equitable way to pay.

Proposed alternatives, such as the mileage tax or using other state funds, are little more than a shell and pea game to enrich the oil and automobile industries.

The gas tax is a "user fee." The more you drive,

the more gasoline you buy, the more tax you pay, and the more you contribute to the maintenance of the roads you use.

There are many reasons why the gasoline tax is not creating enough revenue. Mostly it's the failure to adjust for inflation.

But it's also a good news, bad news story. The good news: the price of gas (with its tax) stimulates (1) higher gas mileage cars and trucks, (2) hybrids, and (3) electric vehicles (along with some other alternatives) – all of which use less gas per mile than cars when the tax was last set.

As a result, we are both emitting fewer greenhouse gases and less dependent on foreign oil.

The bad news: the less gas we use, the less gas tax revenue, the less money we have for roads and bridges.

So why not abandon, or supplement, the gas tax? Because doing so reduces the marketplace incentives for better gas-mileage vehicles. Raising the tax increases those incentives.

For example, paying tax by the mile (instead of by the gallon) there's no tax incentive not to drive a spiffy Hummer (some models get 9 mpg in the city) or inefficient old vehicles. You'll still pay the mileage fee, and more per mile for gas, but no additional gas tax.

Grim reality: we'll either pay for our paved roads or go back to driving on the dirt roads of my youth. Road maintenance costs are more than before. One way or another we're going to pay. That's not the issue. Increasing gas taxes is not an additional outlay that could have been avoided; it's just the best way of paying for it.

My proposal?

Continue to fund road and bridge construction and maintenance with gasoline taxes. Raise the tax rate to whatever's necessary.

Give the more efficient, alternatively-fueled vehicles the gas tax advantages of better gas mileage. Provide what's needed by any new, socially beneficial technology when trying to change culturally embedded habits (such as battery recharging stations for electrics). This is similar to the boost we gave everything from the railroads to the Internet during their early years.

Once the alternative vehicles industries are profitable enough, evaluate several possible approaches for collecting a road user fee from them as well.

But please, think long and hard before abandoning, or diluting, the gasoline tax. Let's not wake up to discover that, "You don't know what you've got until it's gone."

Like Death and Taxes, TIFs and TIFing Seem Here to Stay
Iowa City Press-Citizen, February 3, 2013, p. A7

Considering all the downsides of tax increment financing (TIF), you have to wonder why public officials continue to use it. Is there that much joy in playing

Santa with other people's money?

Whatever the reason, like death and taxes TIFs are here to stay. Officials and their lucky beneficiaries love them, and the public doesn't seem to care – at least not enough to make an organized, political difference.

Nonetheless, it's worthwhile to remind ourselves from time to time why they are such a bad idea. Here's a summary.

1. Roads and schools are traditional government undertakings. Funding private enterprise is not.

2. TIFs are backwards: voters must approve bonds for legitimate public projects, like the justice center, but private TIFs are awarded without public approval, often over taxpayers' objections!

3. They've lost their way. Initially designed for urban renewal and low-income housing, taxpayer-funded TIFs are now used to build upscale condos.

4. It's ideological hypocrisy to praise free markets while coming to city hall tin cup in hand.

5. Telling taxpayers, "I'll keep the profits, you cover the losses," conflicts with capitalism's gamble of risks as well as rewards.

6. TIFs intertwine government and business in something that's neither socialism or capitalism. It's called "corporatism," and combines the worst qualities of both.

7. TIFs distort the market.

8. Even if distortion of market forces was desirable, governments have more effective tools than TIFs that don't require taxpayers' money – zoning regulations and building codes among others.

9. It's inexcusably unfair to fund one business person while leaving his competitors on their own.

10. TIFs take money from schools and other government units, causing either cuts in programs or increased taxes.

11. Even if TIFs would produce taxes many years from now, and they often don't, are ever-increasing taxes (and budgets) an appropriate metric for measuring good government?

12. TIFs aren't needed. There are plenty of investors for sound, profitable business plans. If they and bankers won't fund a project, why should taxpayers?

13. Many TIFed projects would have gone ahead anyway; it's virtually impossible to know if the beneficiary's professed "need" is genuine.

14. All ventures have risk. TIFs have more, because public officials with little business experience and no skin in the game make more mistakes than experienced investors watching their own money.

15. Trying to move businesses from one community to another with competing TIF bribes is a lose-lose strategy.

16. Businesses pick cities for reasons other than TIFs: workforce, local economy, schools, quality of life, transportation, communications infrastructure.

17. Telling officials to TIF "prudently" is as effective as beer ads urging University of Iowa binge drinking students to "drink responsibly." TIFs can be as addictive as alcohol

18. When officials give millions in taxpayers' money to private, for-profit businesses the temptations

for good-old-boy corruption are great – and virtually impossible to uncover.

19. TIFs are, for a taxing authority, what impulse buying is for the rest of us – an expensive, unbudgeted, one-off "I've got to have that!" moment, often followed by buyer's remorse.

20. TIFs can devastate a government's credit rating, thereby increasing the cost of future legitimate projects.

These concerns are relevant for any city.

But Iowa City has another reason to avoid TIFs: We don't need them. Businesses here will thrive; others come because of what we offer. We're ranked near the top of the nation's cities in numerous categories.

I know our officials will continue dropping millions of taxpayers' dollars to the bottom line of for-profit, private ventures. But it still doesn't hurt to ask from time to time, "Why?"

TIF: If You Can't Beat 'Em, Insist on More Transparency
Iowa City Press-Citizen, March 18, 2014, p. A7

I now realize that the dozens of my columns and blog essays over the years, itemizing in detail the evils of TIFs, grew out of a faulty premise.

It is not easy to admit a mistake, especially when one has made it so often. But you are owed that admission – along with a fuller explanation.

We've heard that "seeing is believing." However, it is also true that "believing is seeing." And what my upbringing and early education imbedded in my brain was a belief that colored my vision like the rainbow from a prism in the sun.

And what was that belief? It was that we have a capitalist, free private enterprise, market economy. Oh, sure, we had socialist enterprise as well: the Interstate highway system, national and state parks, libraries, public schools and universities. But business did business and government did government.

Now comes the realization that what I once saw so clearly was but a child of the ignorance born of ideology. It was the believing that made possible my seeing – like the lines from the poem, "Last night I saw upon the stair/A little man who wasn't there." (Hughes Mearns, 1899.)

I was believing in, and seeing, an economy that wasn't there.

That's why TIFs were seen to be an aberration, a cancer simultaneously attacking both capitalism's foundation and taxpayers' pocketbooks. (For numerous links to sources, see "TIFs: Links to Blog Essays," http://fromdc2iowa.blogspot.com/ 2014/03/tifs-links-to-blog-essays.html.)

Like "Amazing Grace," I was blind, but now I see: We don't have a capitalist system. We probably never did.

So how should we describe our economy? The word "fascism" carries too much baggage from World War II – dictators, suppression of opposition, aggressive nationalism, and even racism. "Fascism" doesn't describe America today. But from Washington, D.C., to cities, counties and states across America, in terms of an economy, ours is the economy of fascism.

The more acceptable word today, "corporatism," is less accurate. Because the economy we have is a blend, more resembling a purée than a salad or a stew with identifiable ingredients.

Cities' taxpayers who cannot afford the tickets to an NFL or even college football game invest billions in stadiums, given as gifts to attract the billionaires who own teams of millionaires.

States have multiple funds of taxpayers' money used to compete with other states by giving it away to attract businesses.

Washington is essentially an open bazaar, awash in money gladly given and generously rewarded.

Is this system corrupt? Of course. Welcome to the real world. All economic systems can have corruption – communist, socialist, capitalist, or our fascist.

Is our fascist economy less efficient than a true capitalist economy? Absolutely. Everybody is handling other peoples' money. Is it less humane than a socialist system might be? Of course. When it comes to minimum wages or safer working conditions, our fascist economy is still driven by the belief that "greed is good" – as the character Gordon Gekko's said in the movie "Wall Street."

Folks, in the words Walter Cronkite used to sign off the CBS Evening News, "And that's the way it is." That's the system we have. Get used to it. The beneficiaries love it. The victims don't revolt.

What can we do? Tweak the system. Insist our

governments invest our money rather than giving it away; that they take a share of the ownership – and the profits. Insist on detailed accounting of the return on our money they're investing.

If a fascist economy is wrong, but intractable, we can at least try, as John Carver bemoans in another context, to "do the wrong thing better."

Too Many Negatives, Too Little Upside to TIFs
The Gazette, March 25, 2014, p. A6

Your "The upside of TIFs" (March 15) needed what Paul Harvey used to call "the rest of the story." No one I know argues there has never been any benefit from any tax increment financing deal, anywhere, at any time.

But that's not the issue in a rational benefit-cost analysis.

There are 10 to 20 categories of reasons why all TIFs are a bad idea. (See http://fromdc2iowa.blogspot.com/2014/03/tifs-links-to-blog-essays.html.) And I have yet to see any benefits of TIFs that could begin to outweigh all of those categories of disadvantages.

Here's an analogy:

There would be "a benefit" to letting elementary school students simply roam freely throughout the community without parental supervision or need to attend school. They might better develop their natural curiosity and sense of self-reliance.

But the costs of that proposal – lack of student safety and education among them – would so heavily outweigh its potential benefit that no one seriously would propose it.

So it is with TIFs. An occasional "upside?" Of course. But hardly ever enough to outweigh the multiple downsides.

Talking TIF: Costs Outweigh Possible Benefits
The Gazette, April 13, 2014, pp. A9, A12

There are many reasons why further enriching the backers of for-profit, private ventures with taxpayers' money is a really bad idea.

In 2006 I began a blog. Dozens of its 1000 essays deal with reasons to oppose TIFs. See "TIFs: List of Blog Essays," http://fromdc2iowa.blogspot.com/2014/03/tifs-links-to-blog-essays.html.

Any one of them is reason enough to reject a TIF. To approve it, proponents need to show why none applies.

The issue is not whether a TIF has a single benefit. Benefit-cost analysis requires we total all the costs and burdens of that TIF and weigh them against its individual benefit.

Few if any can pass that test.

Ideological hypocrisy. How can those supporting free private enterprise, capitalism, and marketplace forces, who think "government is the problem" and want it "off their back," justify taking money from the public collection plate?

Anti-democratic. City councils need voters' approval of bonds for legitimate government projects. Yet they can give our money to their friends' private projects on a whim.

Lowered credit rating. TIFs can impact credit ratings. Coralville went from a Moody Aaa credit rating, the highest, to a "lower medium grade" Baa2 in two years.

Opportunity costs. Spending money on one thing costs the lost opportunity to spend it elsewhere. Johnson County Supervisor Rod Sullivan once found a diversion of $700 million of property off the tax rolls. As a result, either we pay more taxes or Supervisors cut needed programs.

Unfairness to neighbors. The TIF-granting body's neighbors often lose out as well — other communities and school districts with less money in their budgets.

Unfairness to competitors. TIFs tilt the playing field. They unfairly upset a free market, punishing honest competitors and benefitting no one except the TIF recipient.

Risky business. Money's always available for good deals. If an entrepreneur, family, friends, investors, venture capitalists, and banks aren't willing to fund a project, maybe taxpayers shouldn't either.

TIFs complicate taxes. We don't deserve more tax complexity and even less transparency.

"Money can't buy love." Why compete with

bribes? A business that needs port access to the Pacific Ocean isn't coming to Iowa. If it did, it would leave for a bigger bribe. Maytag, offered $100 million to stay, left anyway.

TIFs are unnecessary. The Corridor is one of the fastest growing, lowest unemployment areas of Iowa. We already have what businesses want: skilled labor, transportation and communication infrastructure, quality education, cultural attractions and outdoor recreation.

TIF grantors' poor skills, record. The subsidy-grantors' record is not great. Elected officials are more skilled at keeping contributors and constituents happy than at evaluating taxpayer-funded business proposals. TIFed projects have gone belly up, missed deadlines, and new jobs goals. With reasonable follow-up and transparency, we'd know about many more. But TIFs in Iowa have more lenient provisions, and less oversight, than in most other states.

"Need" is unknowable. Many projects will go ahead without subsidy. If tax breaks are available, of course developers will say they need them. Maybe this is blackmail. Maybe they need to look harder for funding. There's no way to know.

At a minimum, here are questions to ask before approving TIFs:

What is this government's past record when we compare promised results with ultimate return or loss?

Why is this project needed?

Why does that need exceed all conventional needs for public funds?

What will other government units lose? How

much more will their taxpayers have to pay?

Of all possible TIF projects, why is this one a top priority?

Who benefits: all citizens, a small segment or primarily the recipient?

How much money is involved?

Why are those who will profit unwilling to invest what is needed? Are their reasons equally applicable to taxpayer funding?

Does the business plan indicate financial success, or reveal risks of failure?

If and when the recipient fails, skips town, goes bankrupt, or misses deadlines, how will taxpayers be protected?

What relationships are there between the potential recipient and the officials approving the funding?

How will the recipient's unfunded private competitors be harmed?

TIFs shouldn't be used at all. If used anyway, let's do the wrong thing better:

Leave the tax code alone. Taxes are taxes, gifts are gifts – through appropriations, fully disclosed and audited.

Don't privatize profits and socialize losses. It's our money. Don't give it. Loan it or invest it. Earn us some interest – with a City or State Bank. Invest our tax money; take an ownership share. Give us at least a gambler's chance at occasional profit. Publicize the details.

We don't have a fascist state, just a fascist economy, government and private enterprise blended to more resemble a purée than a stew with identifiable ingredients.

In Washington, D.C., it's billions of tax dollars; in Des Moines hundreds of millions; in Iowa's cities, TIFs. Without a taxpayer revolt, it's unlikely to change.

Sycamore TIF Unnecessary
Iowa City Press-Citizen, November 23, 2014, p. A5

Hats off to Iowa City Councilor Jim Throgmorton for thinking, speaking and voting rationally regarding his colleagues' generous $1.75 million gift of your money and mine to a Colorado corporation. (It's the second such gift to the Sycamore Mall, after the first proved, once again, that TIFs very often don't deliver on their backers' expectations.)

For 41 previous columns and blog essays detailing a dozen categories of reasons why transferring taxpayers' money to the bottom line of private citizens' for-profit businesses is bad for taxpayers, consumers, competitors of the recipients, the general economy, neighboring communities and governments, see "TIFs: Links to Blog Essays," http://fromdc2iowa.blogspot.com/2014/03/tifs-links-to-blog-essays.html.

And hats off to Andy Davis and the Press-Citizen for not limiting their TIF story ("City Council votes to provide funds to improve Marketplace," Nov. 19) to quotes from council members' swooning over the glories of TIFs. Included within it we find:

"Councilor Jim Throgmorton ... voiced his concerns during the meeting about whether TIF money should be used for the project. 'One normally thinks of a TIF as an incentive. I'm not yet persuaded that the owners need support from the city to take actions that are already in their own economic self-interest.'"

His judgment is supported in another TIF district by two of those bidding for the former St. Patrick Church property. They're also able to profit within a pure capitalist system, with no need for taxpayers' money.

Given our councilors' untreated addiction to TIFs, and their repeated refusals even to acknowledge the harms, they leave voters with no other option than to oppose their re-election.

City is Putting Lipstick on TIFs
Iowa City Press-Citizen, December 2, 2017, p. A6

The City Council is putting lipstick on its TIFs [see, "Andy Davis, "Iowa City Seeks Public Input as it Begins Discussion of Revised TIF Policies," November 18, 2017]. Like new headlights on a rusted-out clunker, it's an improvement, but no reason to buy the car.

There are overwhelming reasons for not putting public money into private, for-profit projects [see, *e.g.*, Nicholas Johnson, "Tussling Over TIFs: Pros and Cons," April 13, 2014, and Nicholas Johnson, "TIFs: Links to Blog Essays," March 16, 2014].

How else can the Council create public benefit? City ownership – like libraries, parks and schools. By applying zoning and building code requirements or new ordinances to private projects.

Iowa City is an economic and cultural magnet. We don't have to bribe new arrivals.

Ah, the argument goes, if we don't play this dirty little game some other city or state will get the business. (They may; but the TIF applicant might also come here without TIFs.)

But what if, as the computer concluded in the movie "War Games," "the only winning move is not to play"? Why do we want more growth and sprawl? What are TIFs' costs as well as benefits?

In 1910 Houston was roughly Iowa City's size today: 79,000. By 2010 it was 2,100,000. How have Houstonians' quality of life improved from two million more people? Would we be happier with two million more neighbors?

That should be the first question.

Vote "No" on Justice Center, But "Yes" for Courthouse
Iowa City Press-Citizen, April 12, 2013, p. A7

There's a happy, win-win approach to Johnson County's courts and jail needs well within reach. Sadly, the County Supervisors didn't grab it.

So I'm voting "No" on the so-called "revised" proposal.

When this vote also fails, let's do what almost everyone agrees on: fix the Courthouse. Detach the jail from both the Courthouse and the ballot proposition. Here's how.

1. Reserve the Courthouse for civil proceedings. Spiff it up. Accommodate ADA requirements and other needs. The Courthouse and Old Capitol are Iowa City's most prized architectural gems.

Relocating criminal proceedings will eliminate much of the Courthouse overcrowding and security concerns, while providing additional offices and space for civil proceedings.

2. Create a detached, stand-alone facility for criminal proceedings and jail cells. It would be much more efficient for those handling criminal cases.

There could be new courtrooms and chambers for judges; offices and rooms for clerks and records, assistant county attorneys, deputy sheriffs, inmates' lawyers and families, training programs, as well as jail cells. They could be designed for optimum efficiency by those using them.

There would be little or no public objection to architectural design. Security could be built in, rather than reconfiguring the Courthouse.

There would be no need to have this facility either near the Courthouse or more than a half-mile away. It would be a one-stop shop; a stand-alone facility.

There is precedent for removing functions from the Courthouse. Offices for all County Departments used to be in the Courthouse. They are now in a separate, County Administration Building a few blocks away with convenient, free parking.

3. There are reasons to preserve the integrity of the Courthouse. The Courthouse, like Old Capitol, is a valuable Iowa City asset. It is an attraction in an area the City wants to develop.

It may be "legal" to attach a modern architectural extension on this 100-year-old U.S. Register of National Historic Places structure, but why would anyone want to do so? Would we put such an extension on Old Capitol? Of course not. We shouldn't want to put one on the Courthouse either. Old Capitol needs its Pentacrest; the Courthouse needs its setting.

Do we want to make the downtown more attractive to potential residents, students and tourists? That appears to be a goal of the downtown merchants, the Chamber of Commerce, the Convention and Visitors Bureau, the City Council, and others.

That being the case, of all the options for housing, entertainment venues, and other attractions south of Burlington, why on earth would we plop jail cells for criminals right in the middle of downtown?

That's nuts.

Particularly since we also despoil an architectural gem of a Courthouse in the process – one that might otherwise actually be an attraction of sorts for those walking or otherwise enjoying the area.

Iowa City is not like Washington, where the best one can hope for is the least worst alternative. We don't have to settle. We can be creative.

We can have it all: improve the Courthouse's interior, while preserving its exterior and setting. Detach a Criminal Justice Center from the ballot, and from the Courthouse; create one more efficient and pleasant to work in than anything dreamed of so far.

Vote "No" May 7th on the unrevised proposal.

Then, later, let's (1) all vote "Yes" for what we do agree on – a refurbished Courthouse; and (2) begin planning, and then agreeing to vote "Yes," on a Criminal Justice Center that will bring deserved distinction to Johnson County.

Getting To "Yes" by Voting "No" on Justice Center
The Daily Iowan, April 30, 2013, p. 4

Dave Parson's ' opinion column urged that we "Vote Yes for the justice center" (DI, April 29). He is a member of the committee actively pushing the proposal. As such, his was a commendably civil, best effort to make the most of his unpersuasive case.

University of Iowa students have a stake in this May 7 bond election, and hopefully, they will vote. Justice-center proponents start from a false premise: Opponents don't understand the need for improvements in our justice-system facilities and procedures.

Not one of my acquaintances opposes the May 7 ballot proposition for that reason. Indeed, quite the contrary. Few, if any, even object to spending whatever taxpayer money we truly need.

No, the dispute doesn't involve whether we need "something" – for reasons Parsons skillfully set forth.

The dispute is what that "something" should be,

how much of it we need, where it should be located, and what reforms in incarceration avoidance should accompany new construction.

I'm not a member of either the "Yes" or the "No" committees. I just want to plan what we need, substantively and procedurally, and do it right, while not making things worse. Like the cable guy says, "let's get 'er done" – get Johnson County voters to "Yes."

Fundamental "getting to 'yes'" strategy involves recognizing the distinction between parties' "positions" and "interests." Proponents and opponents share an "interest" in fixing the system. It's the proponents' "position" that's caused the problem.

Proponents' second logical failing is constructing a position on a conclusion that doesn't follow from their premises: (1) The Courthouse and jail need fixing; (2) We have a detailed specific plan for doing that; (3) Therefore, everyone must vote for our specific plan.

As a law professor might respond to a student's similarly faulty argument, "I follow you all but the 'therefore.'" A need for "something" does not, "therefore," compel adoption of their proposal.

Proponents' stance is reminiscent of the late, former Prime Minister Margaret Thatcher, sometimes called "TINA" because of her response to opponents who proposed alternatives to her policies: "There Is No Alternative" (TINA).

It's like the line from the country song, "That's my story, and I'm sticking to it." "That's our proposal, and we're sticking to it." There is no alternative.

Landfills used to be like that. When one filled, there was no alternative to creating more. Today's acceptance of alternatives – such as recycling and composting – has saved hundreds of acres of farmland.

America leads the world in jail and prison cells. That doesn't mean, when ours fill up, "there is no alternative" to just building more.

It is no less offensive to attach a big-box modern structure to our National Historic Register, 100-year-old Courthouse – as proponents suggest – than attaching a similar structure to the Old Capitol.

Here's one of many alternatives:

Many find a detached, stand-alone criminal justice facility more sensible and efficient – sheriff, judges, courts, and jail in one place. Proponents claim it won't work. Apparently, they failed to tell that to the numerous Iowa counties that have already done it and like it. In fact, it's what we did when we needed more County administrative space: the separate administrative building an easy walk down the street.

This has the added benefits of preserving the integrity of the Courthouse exterior and setting, providing more space inside exclusively for civil proceedings, and avoids plopping a bunch of criminals in jail cells in the center of a downtown area the City would like to develop for tourists and residential use.

If the bond issue passes this time, "that's all she wrote." We'll have to live with a desecrated Courthouse and other consequences. But if it's defeated May 7 maybe, like Goldilocks' porridge tasting, the third time they'll get it right.

There are alternatives.

Still Many More Options for Jail
Iowa City Press-Citizen, May 6, 2013, p. A7

If Tuesday's vote fails, we should vote again.

Proponents proposed a false choice, both in their own thinking and on the ballot.

As a syllogism: (1) We need more jail cells and courthouse refurbishing; (2) We propose specific details to fix that; (3) Therefore, you must vote "Yes" for our plan or be called a naysayer.

The fallacy was their "therefore."

In fact, most opponents agreed on the need to do "something." Disagreement wasn't about need. It focused on the "something": what it is, how much of it, where it should be, and what alternative approaches should accompany construction.

Let's "get to 'Yes.'" There's little debate regarding the courthouse's interior needs. Let's vote on that, approve it and do it.

Then let's give serious consideration to the suggestions from opponents that have largely been rebuffed by the "Yes" crowd. "There Is No Alternative" ("TINA") is no way to reach compromise, whether in Washington, D.C., or Johnson County.

Next steps? Many people have suggestions. Here's mine: Vote to fix the courthouse – for civil trials only.

Design a more efficient, detached, one-stop criminal justice center – as many other Iowa counties have done – to preserve our courthouse's appearance.

Explore and implement all best practices for reducing the need for additional jail and prison cells.

Taxes – 151

There's more at http://FromDC2Iowa.blogspot.com.

Meanwhile, as the Cable Guy says, "Let's get 'er done!"

Residents Deserve Courthouse Annex
Iowa City Press-Citizen, October 28, 2014, p. A7

On Nov. 4 (or before) be sure to vote "yes" on the Courthouse Annex bond proposal.

Opponents of prior proposals wanted alternatives to incarceration, with less recidivism. They wanted a cheaper structure. They wanted to preserve views, and this National Historic Register courthouse's architectural integrity. They wanted a "green" building and accessibility for persons with disabilities.

Well, guess what? The supervisors' response is government at its best. They not only listened, they responded – with everything opponents asked.

Instead of jail cells, they just received a $192,000 grant for their Drug Treatment Court, with employment opportunities for offenders. Building costs are 25 percent less. Views of the courthouse are preserved. It will receive "silver" LEED certification and be ADA compliant.

Supervisors proposing legitimate governmental projects (*e.g.*, courthouses, park acquisition) must get public approval to spend taxpayers' money. Yet city council members who want to give taxpayers' money to their friends' non-governmental, for-profit, private businesses (*e.g.*, luxury condos, grocery stores, motels), can do so while refusing to listen or respond to opponents. Ironic, isn't it?

We need and deserve this courthouse improvement; supervisors deserve our thanks. Vote "yes."

Chapter Six/Technology

Introduction

As a former cyberlaw professor many technology stories attract my attention. Only two inspired columns 2013-2017: the battle over net neutrality (the rules controlling the content, speed, and price of consumers' Internet access) and the perils of texting.

Why Net Neutrality is Our Friend
The Gazette, June 2, 2017, p. A6

President Donald Trump kept his promise. He said he'd "drain the swamp" in Washington. He has. What he didn't tell us was that he would then fill his administration with the creatures that crawled out.

The news media and late-night shows have reveled in their good fortune. Trump has provided them a daily flow of stories both entertaining and terrifying to move their audiences between tears and laughter.

But as a result, that 99 percent-plus of the federal government that's not in the White House is mostly ignored by the media.

Farmers worry over the loss of overseas markets from Trump's trade agreements. Public schools must deal with the loss of revenue from school vouchers. The oil and gas industry cheers a removal of regulations that will enable abuses rivaling the Teapot Dome scandal that sent one of President Warren Harding's cabinet members to prison.

And my old agency, now Trump's Federal Communications Commission, is going about repealing the consumer protection called Network Neutrality. You don't need to know anything about computers or the Internet to understand that one.

You do need to understand monopoly capitalism.

Most cities of any size have an abundant array of restaurants from which to choose – locations, menus, prices, and atmosphere. Aside from health concerns, "marketplace forces" provide adequate consumer protection.

By contrast, with rare exception most neighborhoods in those cities have no choice among monopolist internet service providers, such as Mediacom.

It's the business of business to maximize profits by increasing prices and cutting costs (quality and services) until both reach optimum levels.

In a conversation with University of Chicago economist Milton Friedman he used the example of corporate pollution of rivers. "Nick, you are appealing to them to be ethical," he said. "They can't afford to be ethical. They can afford to comply with a law that's also applicable to their competitors. Your answer is in Congress and state legislatures, not preaching in the streets."

If an Internet service provider (ISP) also profits from distributing content it owns, it can make more money by censoring a competitor's content, charging more for it, or slowing its delivery to your computer or TV. If it doesn't own content providers, it can bargain with those who are, providing them unfair advantages for the right price. And ISPs will set customers' charges at the optimum profit maximizing level.

Harm to consumers will be limited only by the ISPs' imagination.

Once cities have as many ISPs as restaurants we can talk about "marketplace regulation." Meanwhile, common decency requires that the FCC retain the consumer protection of Network Neutrality.

Is Texting the Problem, or Just Part of the Problem?
Iowa City Press-Citizen, June 16, 2014, p. A5

The Press-Citizen thinks we ought to get tougher on DWT – "Driving While Texting." Editorial, "Send Message to Lawmakers About Texting Ban," Iowa City Press-Citizen, June 13, 2014, p. A9. Apparently, law enforcement in Iowa regarding this dangerous practice can only occur once a driver is stopped for something else.

OK, it's hard to argue with the paper's position.

But might we benefit by thinking about this a little longer?

One of the toughest intellectual, linguistic and analytical struggles in addressing a good many challenges is figuring out what it is we are really trying to accomplish, conceptualizing the goal – or as I used to put it to my colleagues on the school board: "How would we know if we were ever 'successful'?"

How a lumber yard owner decides whether to be in the "lumber business" or the "building materials business" can make the difference between profit and loss. Costco and Walmart have decidedly different ideas about how many thousands of items such stores should stock (as well as the impact on profits of paying employees a living wage!). What should be the goal, and measure, of a junior high social studies teacher: the test scores his or her students get in high school social studies classes, the number who go to college and choose social studies-related majors once there? Or should it be how many, five years after graduating, apply what they were taught by registering to vote, actually voting in primaries, school board and city council elections, participating in political parties and campaigns, actually running for office, or becoming what Ralph Nader has called "a public citizen"?

When I was a boy, the speed limit in Iowa was, simply, "reasonable and proper." It might be a little ambiguous, but isn't that really our goal? Is it "reasonable and proper" to drive 55 mph in a 55 mph zone when the early morning fog still hangs heavily over a very icy road? Of course not.

Similarly, is it really texting that is the problem? Isn't texting just a part of the problem – one that no one could have anticipated 20 years ago? If we'd like to be a little more precise than "reasonable and proper," but less specific than "texting," and we'd like a word that eliminates the need to constantly revise the law as new technology comes along, how about "DWD" – "driving while distracted"?

Isn't that the problem? Whatever your confidence

about your "multi-tasking" abilities, it is impossible to compose (or read) text on a handheld device and keep your eyes on the road at the same time. But your driving suffers the same impairment regardless of the cause of the distraction: driving while shaving or putting on makeup, reading the paper, changing stations on the radio, turning around to watch kids in the back seat, looking on the floor of the car for the quarter or toll road ticket you dropped, figuring out your location on your GPS device, even concentrating on a serious hands-free phone conversation – or an intense conversation with a passenger in the car.

Shouldn't this be our legislative, and editorial, focus – DWD, "driving while distracted," what many claim is as hazardous as DWI.

158 – Columns of Democracy

Chapter Seven/War

Introduction

President Dwight Eisenhower warned us of "the military-industrial complex" in his 1961 "Farewell Address." There has been little if any improvement since. U.S. military expenditures far exceed those of the next five or ten nations combined, with financial records that can't be audited and as much as a trillion dollars unaccounted for. We have a military presence in some 150 countries and are seemingly always fighting wars somewhere – some "wars of choice" and others perpetual wars (compared with World War II's resolution in four years). This chapter contains columns with thoughts about these challenges, along with the allied issues involving "terrorism" and what to do with the refugee populations for which we bear some responsibility.

The Militarization of America
The Gazette, July 5, 2015, p. C3

Text [in brackets] was submitted to The Gazette, included in its online version, but omitted from its hard copy edition.

Philadelphia police crowd control 30 years ago? Dropping a bomb from a helicopter; 60 homes burned.
Not the typical response of the thousands who do "protect and serve." But today's militarization of local

police with hand-me-down Army equipment is worth examining – in context.

Because it's only a small part of the militarization of America.

We are the world's pre-eminent military power. Of the top ten military nations we spend more than the other nine combined. With our military presence in over 150 countries, and provision of weapons to others, we have militarized the world.

Expenditures reflect values. There is little political objection to the trillions of debt from credit card military adventures. We accept the opportunity costs as we reject universal, single-payer health care, starve our public schools, cut programs for the poor, and watch our infrastructure crumble. "We're number one!" we cry, notwithstanding low international rankings for test scores, infant mortality, and life expectancy.

Our national anthem celebrates "the rockets' red glare, the bombs bursting in air." Our sporting events often begin with a vocalist and spectators singing that song. Athletic contests in many cultures serve, in part, to prepare young men for battle. Our most popular sport is our most violent: football. Those games sometimes begin with a flyover of military fighter planes.

We have a ["ready, fire, aim"] militarized media, its cheerleaders for war ready to support every military action. [Never mind we haven't been attacked, and there's no realistic threat.] War coverage is dramatic and improves ratings, whether baby wars (Granada), "preemptive" wars (Iraq), or perpetual wars elsewhere. [TV stations used to "sign off" at night with visuals of flags and fighter planes. As Mason Williams said,

"Every night, before it goes to bed, television gets down on its knees and prays to war."]

We have militarized our homes and ourselves. Our children play with video games that train them as military sharpshooters and drone operators. Roughly 40 percent are living in homes with guns. The U.N. reports America's gun death risk per 100,000 population is 20 times the average for other countries.

There are 50,000 suicides and homicides each year; 60 percent involve guns. (Homicide is the second leading cause of death for those 15-25 years old.) Some estimate guns in homes are 16 times more likely to harm occupants than intruders.

Given those odds, Americans must really love their guns a lot – a love that surpasses all understanding.

It's natural such a nation would have a National Rifle Association (NRA) opposing virtually every form of gun regulation, including retention of databases of gun purchases, background checks on purchasers at gun shows, changes in the registration of firearms, and restrictions on sales of assault weapons,.

With the expansion of permits to carry we see the militarization of other institutions as well. There are guns on college campuses, in schools, malls, movie theaters, bars and even churches. And there are the all-too-regular reports of deaths – genuinely grieved, but all too quickly forgotten.

We have militarized our politics and governing. Few elected officials are defeated for supporting increased defense appropriations or the NRA's agenda. Many have military bases or defense contractors in their districts. Coupled with the NRA's campaign contributions, large membership, and ability to defeat its opponents, military-industrial complex and NRA victories are not surprising.

We've already militarized law enforcement.

The 1878 Posse Comitatus Act makes it a federal crime to use "any part of the Army ... to execute the laws." However, with many exceptions plus the Insurrection Act it's a low hurdle.

In 1932, President Hoover ordered Army General Douglas MacArthur and Major Dwight Eisenhower to use the infantry to remove the WWI Bonus March veterans from their Mall encampments. President Eisenhower used the Army's 101st Airborne Division to integrate the Little Rock schools in 1957. When riots followed Dr. King's 1968 assassination, President Johnson ordered 2,000 82nd Airborne Division paratroopers flown to Washington.

Sometimes Army intervention aids big business. In the 1921 Battle of Blair Mountain, President Warren Harding ordered the Army to support mine owners against 10,000 miners. Since the 1890s union organizing and strikes have often yielded to government force – including the Army.

In October 2002, the activation of USNORTHCOM marked the first time since George Washington that a military commander's mission is our own homeland.

Militarized nations need blanket surveillance of their civilians. We have that, too. The NSA plus 15 other spy agencies we know about.

That's the context. Now let's talk about the

militarization of police.

Spending on Military Always Comes at a Cost
The Gazette, April 9, 2917, p. D5

My father grew up on a Kansas cattle farm in the early 20th Century. Times were tough, and so were parents. He recalled sitting on the porch steps at a neighbor's farm house when that farmer's young, barefoot boy approached and asked for a nickel. The boy's father answered, "What did you do with the last nickel I gave you?"

It's much easier these days for America's military. Often it doesn't even need to ask. Elected officials sometimes send additional taxpayers' money its way for the weapons systems of major campaign donors, weapons the military would really rather not have, thank you.

As for "the last nickel I gave you," the General Accounting Office has often just thrown up its hands in frustration and announced that the military's financial records are in a condition that simply makes audits impossible.

So estimates vary, but most agree we are spending on our military more than the next nine nations combined – much of which is used to make sure that we could win should we ever have to fight World War II all over again. Unfortunately, there's little that the President Gerald Ford $8-to-13 billion aircraft carrier can do to defend us from cyber attacks or terrorists' random, homemade bombs.

Throw in the cost of caring for the wounded (Department of Veterans Affairs), and other costs throughout the federal budget, and the military's share of federal discretionary spending is well over the 54% just going to the Pentagon. (Estimates of the costs of our wars in Afghanistan and Iraq alone, among the most difficult to audit, range between one and five trillion dollars.)

It's hard enough for most of us to deal with things measured in the millions of dollars. We can't even imagine how we should evaluate costs in the billions and trillions of dollars.

So let's just focus on the cost of one operation, during one day (yesterday, April 7), involving missile strikes on one Syrian Airforce base.

It required 59 Tomahawk Cruise missiles. At $1.4 million per missile that's $82.6 million.

So how much is $82.6 million?

Think of it this way: Given the median income of Iowa's K-12 teachers, $82.6 million would be enough to pay the salaries of over 1700 additional teachers for one year – roughly a 5% increase in the number of Iowa's 35,000 teachers.

That's something we can imagine.

Now multiply that by roughly 10,000 times and you'll have some notion of how much our military expenditures are denying us in health care, jobs programs, education, infrastructure improvements, and other pro-people social programs.

Think about what President Eisenhower's

military-industrial complex did with the last nickel you gave it. Think about it – and act.

Is War the Best Answer?
Iowa City Press-Citizen, September 12, 2014, p. A7

> *We must anticipate and be prepared for the unintended consequences of our action.... As we weigh our options, we should be able to conclude with some confidence that the use of force will move us toward the intended outcome.*
> – General Martin Dempsey, Chair, Joint Chiefs of Staff, July 19, 2013

With his speech Wednesday evening, once again an American President is preparing the people for a rush to war in Iraq – adding Syria to our expanding battlefield.

Once again, our oil has found its way under someone else's sand.

Once again, we must turn to our military leaders for the caution and rational analysis borne of their experience in battle and their study of history.

Now I'm not saying the pre-election threat to America from ISIS in President Obama's scenario is no more serious today than the pre-election threat to America from Albania was in the movie "Wag the Dog." Those ISIS folks seem a truly brutal lot.

But the intelligence community is much less

alarmist than the politicians and pundits. As National Counterterrorism Center Director Matthew G. Olsen put it last week, "ISIL is not Al Qaeda pre-9/11." Homeland Security Secretary Jeh C. Johnson agrees: "We know of no credible information that ISIL is planning to attack the homeland at present."

Moreover, the President's strategy carries high risk of creating the very threat that does not now exist. Former National Counterterrorism Center Deputy Director Andrew Liepman says, "It's pretty clear that upping our involvement in Iraq and Syria makes it more likely that we will be targeted by the people we are attacking."

Put aside for the moment any moral questions about the inevitable deaths of thousands of civilians. Put aside legal questions about the President's authority to wage this war, and international law restraints on "preemptive war." Put aside the likelihood that our intervention will increase, rather than decrease, ISIS' recruitment of terrorists and risk of harm to our homeland. Put aside the multi-trillion-dollar cost for our grandchildren of these Mideast adventures.

What is our goal? The President says it is to "degrade and ultimately destroy" ISIS. What if the Iraqi Army is not up to that task? What's "Plan B"? Do we go home, or send in American troops? Are we better off once we've destroyed the Syrian government's toughest enemy?

Have we "destroyed" al Qaeda or just moved it off the front page? Assume we destroyed al Qaeda. How did that work out for us? We got ISIS. Do we really think if we could destroy ISIS nothing would replace it?

What's our exit strategy? Once we "win," how do we get out, and what happens when we do? Even if we could eliminate today's chaos, tribalism, ethnic and religious conflict, why will it not return?

The most fundamental question that's seldom if ever stated, let alone addressed or resolved is, "What is our ultimate goal, our purpose, for this air war in Iraq and Syria?" As I used to put it to my school board colleagues, "How would we know if we'd ever been successful?" Hopefully, our purpose is not limited to executing our "strategy" for winning battles and wars so we can then come home, leaving the survivors to fend for themselves.

Will we clean up after the party, reconstructing what war destroys? For how long? With how many billions of taxpayers' dollars? Is nation-building still a part of our Mideast mission?

Even though we're rightfully enraged over the beheadings, and want to "do something," unthinking, precipitous action is not always the most effective revenge.

Six Step Program for Avoiding War
Iowa City Press-Citizen, November 11, 2014, p. A7

It's too late to challenge President Obama's recent doubling of U.S. troops in Iraq

But it may be the right time to rethink America's approach to war.

The Pew Research Center's Andrew Kohut reports "the public feels little responsibility and inclination to deal with international problems that are not seen as direct threats to the national interest."

Yet too many of our Washington politicians are like the small boy with a hammer who thinks everything he encounters needs pounding. Spending more on our military than the rest of the world combined, war becomes their first rather than last resort.

This approach to foreign policy consumes trillions of taxpayers' dollars, billions in rebuilding costs, creates millions of homeless refugees, kills hundreds of thousands of innocent civilians, wounds and kills thousands of American soldiers, and decreases our national security by increasing Islamic State's recruitment of angry terrorists from 80 countries.

America won World War II in four years. Our current wars last three times as long with nothing yet approaching "Mission Accomplished."

The computer in the 1983 movie "War Games," in its countdown to "Global Thermonuclear War" finally concludes that, like tic-tac-toe, "The only winning move is not to play."

Can't we learn, in a dozen years, what that computer figured out in a dozen seconds? The best, and sometimes only, way to win a war is to avoid it.

Here's a six-step program for doing that.

Citizen Involvement. Consider a draft, and other World War II-style citizen sacrifice. It's not only a winning strategy; increased citizen involvement is a more democratic strategy. Potential Viet Nam War draftees were the backbone of that war's citizen protest. After 9/11, we were told to "go shopping." Today less than 1 percent of us fight wars about which the rest of us know little and care less, compared with the 16 million who went into WWII.

Pay-As-You-Go. Stop putting the cost of wars on a credit card left to our grandchildren. A supplementary war tax would focus citizen and congressional attention on the financial realities of war, while reducing national debt.

Accountability. Make every senator and member of Congress cast a recorded vote, yes or no, before starting or escalating wars – as our Constitution envisioned.

UN Force. When our national interests aren't involved, shift responsibility for humanitarian military interventions to a United Nations rapid deployment force.

Discussion. Authorization for the human genome project mandated review of the ethical, legal and social issues (ELSI) it raised. War involves more than military considerations. It deserves mass media giving voice to America's best independent minds, and public discussion of the ethical, legal, social, cultural, economic, medical, international relations and many other issues raised by war.

Check list. There are also military issues. Military leaders, more than politicians, wisely insist on answers before committing troops. We should, too.

What's the problem, or challenge? What's our goal? Is it sufficiently important, clearly defined, and understood? Why will military force contribute to, rather than impede, its accomplishment? What possibly more effective non-military alternatives are there?

What are the benefits and costs, gains and losses, risks and rewards? What will it require in troops, materiel, lives, and treasure? How long will it take? Are the American people and their congress supportive? How about the local population where we'll be fighting? Do we know their language, culture, history, tribal and social structure? What are the metrics for evaluating if we're "successful"? What, then, is our exit strategy? After we leave, will things be better than now, the same, or become progressively worse?

Sometimes, regretfully, war may be the only choice. But the thesis of this six-step program is that, if we were to follow it, we would be less likely to leap into ill-considered, unwinnable, counterproductive military actions, and more likely to succeed in those that cannot be avoided.

Syria's Refugees: Job One and Job Two
The Gazette, November 1, 2015, p. C4

> *I didn't think we could just sit here idly and say, "Let those people die." We wouldn't want the rest of the world to say that about us if we were in the same situation. Do unto others as you'd have them do unto you.*
> *– Iowa's Governor Robert D. Ray, welcoming Vietnamese, Cambodian, and Laotian immigrants, 1975 (post Viet Nam War)*

In March, 2011, Syria's President Assad fired on peaceful Syrian, Arab Spring demonstrators. By July the demonstrators were joined by defectors from Assad's army who renamed themselves the Free Syrian Army and were engaged in a civil war. Soon Iran was supporting Assad; Saudi Arabia and other Gulf States came to the aid of the rebels.

Five years later, it has become a regional version of a World War III. In addition to Syria, it involves the countries of Iran, Iraq, Jordan, Lebanon, Saudi Arabia, Turkey – and now Russia and the United States, among others. Other state-like groups include al Qaeda in Syria, Hezbollah, ISIS, Kurds, the anti-Assad rebels – plus another 100 factions – all of which switch sides and membership from time to time. Then there is the Islamic division, with Sunnis supporting the rebels and Shiites supporting Assad.

Nearly a quarter-million Syrians have been killed – most of whom were innocent civilians neither wishing for nor participating in this war. There are uncounted millions who have been injured, deprived of food or health care, and are missing family members. Homes and businesses have been destroyed, as have entire cities, leaving many without shelter or access to supplies.

The UN estimates 7.6 million Syrians (out of a pre-war population of 23 million) are now displaced within Syria, in addition to the 4 million Syrian refugees who have been able to leave. What should be the obligations of the warring countries creating their pain?

Few if any of us have ever experienced anything remotely like what they have been through and continue to experience.

But as we try to imagine what it must be like, one cannot watch the news of their lives, whether in Syria, or on their way elsewhere, and not be emotionally moved. What can we Iowans do to help from halfway around the world?

Iowans, like Americans in the other 49 states, have been and continue to be enriched by the diversity and skills of our new arrivals. The UI alone has students from 112 countries. And as the opening quote from former Governor Robert Ray reveals, Iowa has a proud history of welcoming those in need of a new home during Iowa's recent, as well as its early years.

So it's pretty clear what those of us within the Gazette's circulation area can and should do. We need to encourage our public officials to continue Iowa's tradition – the presidential candidates, our Governor, legislators, county supervisors, and city council members. We need to work from within our churches, social service agencies, civic clubs and other organizations to build consensus – and collaboration – encouraging and preparing for their arrival.

That's today's job one in this crisis.

But job two still looms: trying to learn from this experience what America has apparently been unable to learn from our unwelcome military incursions into Viet Nam, Afghanistan, and Iraq – among many other countries.

The West created the Middle East. In May 1916, Mark Sykes (British), and Francois Georges-Picot (French), with Russia's knowledge, came to a secret understanding to demolish the Ottoman Empire and draw new boundaries for French and British-administered areas.

World War III is not World War II. "Terrorism" is not a nation. If we wanted to treat it as such after 9/11 we should have been bombing and invading Saudi Arabia rather than Afghanistan and Iraq – since that's where the money and airline hijackers came from. Our incursions have created more terrorists than have been killed.

The computer WOPR (War Operation Plan Response) in the movie "War Games" ultimately called off a thermo-nuclear war between the U.S. and Russia after being frustrated by its inability to win at tic-tack-toe. As it concluded, "the only winning move is not to play." We have not been as wise as that computer.

The answer? It can fit on a bumper sticker: "Whatever is the question, war is not the answer."

Sober Risk Assessment Needed to Respond to Terror
Iowa City Press-Citizen, November 28, 2015, p. A11

There's so much craziness involved in our response to "terrorism," and potential Syrian refugees. Where to begin?

Let's start with risk assessment.

It turns out that someone with a fear of dying in a terrorist attack is like a two-pack-a-day cigarette smoker with a fear of flying.

About 3000 people died in the Twin Towers collapse, September 11, 2001. But that number die every month of every year from guns. An equal number die every month in automobiles. Over 7000 die every month from alcohol related causes. Tobacco contributes to 40,000 deaths a month – a risk for our cigarette smoker 10,000 or more times greater than airlines.

Your risks from the most bizarre accident you can imagine is greater than your risk of a terrorist act.

Will we have more U.S. radical jihadist terrorist attacks? Probably; mostly home grown. Can we stop all of them? Of course not. Would more NSA surveillance of Americans help? Probably not. There was advance intelligence about terrorists' suspicious flight training, and Osama bin Laden's intention to strike New York. The Russians told us about the Boston Marathon bombers. ISIS' attacks in Paris were masterminded by someone well known to authorities. Making the haystack bigger doesn't make the needle easier to find.

It has been suggested that we admit Christians from Syria, but not Muslims – indeed that all U.S. Muslims be issued identity cards and entered in a database.

There are so many things wrong with such violations of our values and Constitution. We don't punish religions. Moreover, if we're going to do it anyway, we need to single out Christians not Muslims. Christians have committed multiples more domestic terrorist acts than Muslims.

When emotions run high, we need to recall our shame at refusing to welcome German Jewish refugees before World War II. Provoked by politicians, Americans' fear the Jews might be communists caused our government to turn the Jews' boats around and send them back to their death at the hands of Nazis.

If we're going to respond to events in Paris with anything beyond what we're already doing, refusing to take Syrian refugees is one of the worst things we could do. Not only will it fail to make us safer, it will help to make ISIS stronger.

Focusing on Syrians rather than Europeans is like focusing on Afghans after planeloads of Saudis, funded by other Saudis, brought down the Twin Towers. Not only were the Paris bombers Europeans, not Syrians, as such they could easily enter the U.S. as tourists.

Nearly 35 million foreigners visit our country every year – many don't even need visas. If we don't fear admitting those 35 million, without vetting them, by what logic do we refuse to take 10,000 Syrians who have gone through years of the most intense vetting imaginable?

Since 9/11 we have admitted 785,000 refugees into our country. During those 14 years only three have been arrested on terrorism-related charges. That's 0.0004 of 1 percent. There's no credible reason to believe our vetting of Syrians will be significantly less successful.

Over 10 million Syrians have left their homes. Europe has welcomed them. We can't accept 1/10th of 1% of that number?

Bear in mind, ISIS is not trying to take over our 3 million square miles or kill our 300 million people. This is not your grandfather's war. ISIS is just trying to terrorize us, to make us fearful. When we build more chain-link fences and hire more security guards, when we can't enter an airplane – or even a college football stadium – without being frisked or x-rayed, they've won.

Our military presence in the Middle East has helped them recruit far more suicide bombers than we've ever killed. And our leaving Syria's young people with no option but to join ISIS will do the same.

What Motivates "Terrorist Thugs"?
The Gazette, December 20, 2015, p. C4

Also as, Understanding Terrorist Thugs, The Daily Iowan, December 3, 2015, p. A4

What is the ultimate goal of those terrorist thugs in Iraq and Syria with their random, if organized, attacks on innocent Westerners?

Until we figure that out, our responses run a serious risk of making us less, rather than more, safe.

Here's a possible explanation.

In their minds, this is not a battle against the West as an ultimate goal. It is a battle for the hearts and minds of the world's 1.5 billion Muslims, designed to bring them into the thugs' ambit. To achieve this, they need two things. They need evidence the West is in fact waging a war on Islam that puts all Muslims in danger. And they need plausibly to argue they offer Muslims protection from hostile Westerners. Where? In a state of their own, their Islamic Caliphate (Arabic for "successor;" in this case successor to the Prophet

Mohammed).

To do this they want and need war with the West. Like a bully looking for a fight, terrorist acts that provoke our response of war serve their cause. What better evidence of a war than our organizing coalitions, bombing their territory, and sending in troops? When our leaders oblige, and then call this a "war" or "clash of cultures" they just help the terrorists' cause.

When our governors refuse to accept suffering Syrian refugees or say we should admit Christian but not Syrian Muslims, it further confirms the thugs' case. When Muslims needing our protection are rejected by us, we leave them no option but to look to these thugs for protection.

We further aid their cause when we buy into the assertion that they do, in fact, control a state, using the reference they prefer: "Islamic State" (in the acronyms ISIS and ISIL).

That is why the name used here is "terrorist thugs" rather than any mention of their "state."

Do they enjoy killing Westerners, by whatever means? Yes. They probably even get a chuckle from our seeming inability to find them with our global, industrial-grade surveillance – and then when we do, our failures to use and share the results.

But it's highly unlikely they share Hitler's vision of taking over the territory of Europe and the United Sates or killing us all. Their goal does not require, nor do they have, such resources. That's why they welcome our providing the video images of a war waged inside their state. Meanwhile, their public-relations media experts are tasked with the global distribution of recruiting material, along with claims of credit for events such as the downed Russian airliner and the coordinated Paris killings.

We calmly accept 30,000 gun deaths every year as our constitutional right, but panic at the prospect of up to 1/10th of 1 percent more killings from terrorist acts. We erect buildings' physical barriers, increase military and police presence, search fans at college football stadiums, and perform a theater of ineffective "security" in airports. Since the thugs' provocations involve terrorism rather than war, every time we appear terrorized more points are put up on their scoreboard.

Suppose a traditional war could be fought there, with a uniformed enemy, and frontlines on battlefields (rather than killing innocents in urban warfare). Even if we won, what then? Why would it be any different from the last time, when we imposed a Shiite government on the formerly ruling Sunnis, chaos reigned, and the opportunist Sunni tribal leaders looked to the thugs for stability?

Some of these tribes have hundreds, even thousands, of years of history. The last time they helped us, we turned our backs and left them to struggle. Why should they trust us now?

But they may be our only hope. Fighting terrorism is like a game of whack-a-mole. The more we kill the more recruits they get. New thugs-in-chief replace the old. Tribal leaders are our only long-term hope. In Iraq, all wars as well as politics are local.

Focus on Muslims Misplaced After Shooting
Iowa City Press-Citizen, June 17, 2016, p. A5

Also: "Focus on Muslims Misplaced After Shooting," Iowa City Press-Citizen (online), June 16, 2016. This column is a response to Ian Goodrum, "Finger-Pointing After Orlando Massacre," Iowa City Press-Citizen, June 15, 2016, p. A9.

Ian Goodrum has reminded us, with writing befitting our City of Literature, of both the causes of the home-grown mass violence in Orlando, and how such tragedies are seized upon by those promoting political or other causes. ("Finger Pointing After Orlando Massacre," June 15.)

He notes the killers' "common denominator" is that they are "young, angry men," and then provides insight into the pathology of their anger.

Among those promoting causes, he observes, are "bloodthirsty pundits and politicians" now calling "for state-sponsored discrimination against believers in Islam, along with a general ramping up of our military presence in the Middle East."

Goodrum's right on all counts, as I see it. Our enemy is not Islam. It's a few of our home-grown, American "young, angry men." These individuals are mostly citizens, with a diversity of histories, persuasions, mental conditions, motives, weapons and targets. They're not all Muslims. More domestic hate crimes involve perpetrators who would claim to be Christian than Muslim. Their targets are no more predictable than where a lightning strike may hit –

federal buildings, universities, African-American churches, gathering spots for Latinos, Asians, Mormons, Catholics, Jews and the LGBT community.

To reduce mass violence, we must focus on our young, angry men. Our mission: to treat their anger before we have to treat their victims.

That is but one of the reasons why focusing on Muslims is counterproductive. Even if it were not unconstitutional and inhospitable, as President Barack Obama points out, it is precisely what ISIS wants us to do – confirm ISIS' assertion that we have declared war on Islam and its 1.6 billion followers, giving an enormous boost to their recruiting.

The "bloodthirsty pundits and politicians" who think more troops and bigger bombs are the answer are clearly not our friends. This is a high-stakes whack-a-mole drama in which all the world is ISIS' stage, where for every bomb we drop more actors come on stage to respond with creative acts of violence.

ISIS has proven creative and adaptable. When we X-ray passengers for guns, they switch to plastic shoe bombs. When they lose a city, they move elsewhere. When they begin to lose on every battlefield, they invite and train terrorists to execute ISIS-orchestrated slaughter in Europe and elsewhere. When the West's capability to track their messages, movements, and money begins to interfere with such organized efforts, they need a new strategy.

Here it is.

Our State Department describes Abu Muhammed al-Adnani as the "official spokesman and a senior leader of Isis." In September 2014 he used ISIS' sophisticated communications networks to propagate the following message:

"If you can kill a disbelieving American or European, French, an Australian or a Canadian, then rely upon Allah, and kill him. Smash his head with a rock, or slaughter him with a knife, or run him over with your car, or throw him down from a high place. Don't try to communicate with us. Don't expect our help, he said. Just do the killing, and pledge allegiance to ISIS."

Since that time, in each of those named countries, there have been killings that used these itemized means of murder, followed by declarations of allegiance to ISIS, there have been killings.

Goodrum is right that the Orlando shooting wasn't the result of "direct involvement or orchestration by" ISIS; as were Orlando officials' conclusions the shooter wasn't a "member of ISIS." But ISIS' latest strategy may have been at play.

None of which changes the numbers. One day in Orlando, 49 were gunned down. But every day in the U.S., nearly 100 are killed with guns. An Islamophobic focus on this carnage is both self-defeating and close to statistically irrelevant.

Meanwhile, somebody better tell those "bloodthirsty pundits and politicians" who didn't get the memo that they're three strategies behind ISIS, running a trillion-dollar program as old as Windows 95.

Is Boston Bomber's Photo Worth 11,000 Words?
Iowa City Press-Citizen, July 20, 2013, p. A10

One hundred years ago next month, the Piqua (Ohio) Leader-Dispatch carried an ad for the Piqua Auto Supply House containing the phrase, "One Look Is Worth A Thousand Words." It's considered a source for the oft-heard expression, "A picture is worth a thousand words."

What Rolling Stone magazine has discovered with its Aug. 1 issue is: The picture that can substitute for 1,000 words can also destroy, in this case, over 11,000 words of first-rate journalism about Dzhokhar ("Jahar") Tsarnaev and the April 15 Boston bombing.

The author, Janet Reitman, is an accomplished, award-winning investigative feature writer with 20 years experience, including Rolling Stone magazine. Her most recent book is The New York Times bestseller "Inside Scientology" (2011).

Few have criticized her Rolling Stone story. It would be hard to do so. She's uncovered and provided as much detail and understanding as anyone could about Tsarnaev and what caused him to do what he did.

But Walgreens and CVS have taken the magazines out of their stores. Why? They don't like Tsarnaev's picture on the cover. It is, not incidentally, the very picture that appeared on the front page of The New York Times Sunday edition on May 5.

Of course, stores have the legal right to choose what magazines they sell. But it's hard to understand, let alone approve of, these corporations' censorship actions. They are reminiscent of Nazi book burning, or Taliban reactions to pictures of Muhammad, and reveal a profound ignorance of the informative role of journalism in a democracy.

Time magazine put Adolf Hitler on its cover, as Person of the Year, in 1938; Joseph Stalin was similarly honored twice (1939, 1942). Each was responsible for orders of magnitude more deaths than Tsarnaev ever planned.

Rolling Stone was scarcely honoring the bomber, let alone declaring him the Person of the Year. The front page of the online version of the Aug. 1 Rolling Stone headlines the top story, "Jahar: The Making of a Monster." The inside subhead reads, in part, "no one saw the pain he was hiding or the monster he would become." Neither reads like the wording of a publicist working for Tsarnaev.

Rolling Stone's editors explain, "The fact that Dzhokhar Tsarnaev is young, and in the same age group as many of our readers, makes it all the more important for us to examine the complexities of this issue and gain a more complete understanding of how a tragedy like this happens."

The Boston Globe editorializes, "Readers shouldn't assume that a cover story about a suspected evildoer represents an attempt to glamorize him. This issue of Rolling Stone should be judged not by its cover, but on the information that it brings to the public record."

Boston Mayor Thomas M. Menino said

Tsarnaev's picture "rewards a terrorist with celebrity treatment." The police commissioner, Edward Davis, declared himself "disgusted by it."

Danielle Marcus, CVS's public relations manager, offered this explanation: "As a company with deep roots in New England and a strong presence in Boston, we believe this is the right decision out of respect for the victims of the attack and their loved ones." Walgreens' Tweet read simply, "Walgreens will not be selling this issue of Rolling Stone magazine."

Americans need that picture and story – because Tsarnaev is what bombers look like. Neither Middle East wars abroad nor NSA spying at home can save us. What perhaps could help is trying to understand American citizens like Jahar in Boston and McVeigh in Oklahoma City.

About the Author

Nicholas Johnson was born and raised in Iowa City, Iowa (1934-1952). He holds undergraduate and law degrees from the University of Texas, Austin. Following graduation, he clerked for U.S. Fifth Circuit Court of Appeals Judge John R. Brown and U.S. Supreme Court Justice Hugo L. Black. After teaching at the University of California, Berkeley, law school and practicing with Covington & Burling, Washington, President Lyndon Johnson appointed him U.S. Maritime Administrator. He is best known for his tumultuous seven-year term as a commissioner of the Federal Communications Commission. Until his recent retirement (2014) he was teaching at the University of Iowa College of Law, having returned from Washington to his hometown in 1980 and boyhood family house in 1989. He has travelled widely and played a variety of roles: congressional primary candidate and school board member; author, columnist, and public lecturer; corporate lawyer and public interest advocate; TV host and radio commentator; and a public health policy institute co-director. In 2009 he was included in *The Yale Biographical Dictionary of American Law* as one of 700 individuals described by the publisher as "leading figures in the history of American law, from the colonial era to the present day." Website and contact information: https://www.nicholasjohnson.org. Blog: https://FromDC2Iowa.blogspot.com.

186 – Columns of Democracy

Cover Photo Credits

MEDIA – New York Times office building
Link: https://commons.m.wikimedia.org/wiki/File:Nytimes_hq.jpg
Author: Haxorjoe
Date: December 23, 2007 4:02:25 p.m.
License: Creative Commons Attribution-Share Alike 3.0 Unported license
https://creativecommons.org/licenses/by-sa/3.0/

EDUCATION – Old Capitol, University of Iowa, Iowa City, Iowa
Link: https://AboutGregJohnson.com/ photography/old-capitol
Author: Gregory Johnson
Date: May 7, 2015, 3:20 p.m.
License: Creative Commons Attribution-Share Alike 3.0

JUDICIARY—U.S. Supreme Court
Link: https://commons.wikimedia.org/wiki/File:United_States_Supreme_Court_Building_on_a_Clear_Day.jpg
Author: Sunira Moses
Date: September 22, 2014, 12:16 p.m.
License: Creative Commons Attribution-Share Alike 3.0 Unported license

188 – Columns of Democracy

VOTING – Worthington Center, Massachusetts, Town Hall and Polls
Link: https://commons.wikimedia.org/wiki/File:Town_Hall,Worthington_Center_MA.jpg
Author: John Phelan
Date: August 30, 2009
License: Creative Commons Attribution-Share Alike 3.0 Unported

LIBRARIES – Iowa City Carnegie Public Library (1904)
Link: https://dsps.lib.uiowa.edu/clip/library/iowa-city/
Author: Unknown
Date: unknown
Permission: Carnegie Libraries in Iowa Project (CLIP), Digital Scholarship & Publishing Studio, School of Library and Information Science, University of Iowa, Dr. Shana Stuart, Director

Back cover photo of Nicholas Johnson
Photo credit: Andrea Chapman Day
https://www.facebook.com/chappieday
Used with permission.

Index

Advice and Consent, 107
Afghanistan, 164
al Adnani, Abu Mohammed, 180
al Assad, Bashar, 171
alcohol
   21-only, 57, 58, 59
   addiction, 82
   bars in business of profiting from, 57, 58
   binge drinking, 95
   consumption as human rights issue, 57, 59
   deaths from, 174
   excessive consumption, 78
   prohibition, 67
   provides football, what bacon does for McDonald hamburgers, 69
ALEC, 38
Alinsky, Saul, 105, 116
Alston, Philip, 122, 123
Amazing Grace, 136
Ames, Iowa, 55
analytics, 86

Money Ball movie, 86
Arkansas, 51
Bahai Universal House of Justice, 94
Banaji, Mahzarin, 92
Barta, Gary, 69, 70, 71
benefit-cost analysis, 67, 137
Bentsen, Lloyd, 105
Bernstein, Carl, 88
best practices, 74, 151
bicycling
   multiple benefits of, 95
Biden, Joe, 87, 88
bin Laden, Osama, 174
Blankfein, Lloyd, 21
Blum, Rod, 112
Booth, Heather, 116
Bork, Robert, 107
Boston, 174, 182, 183, 184
   analytics, 87
Boston Globe, 183
Branstad, Terry, 38, 112
Brazil, 47
Brennan, William J., 73
Bush, George H.W., 113
Bush, George W., 113

California, 31, 33, 43, 44, 51, 54, 81
  economic growth and education, 49
  economy, 49
Carver, John, 137
CBS, 137
Cedar Falls, Iowa, 55
Census Bureau, 79
Chicago, 48, 116, 118
  education, tuition free community college, 49
Chomsky, Noam, 21
Christie, Chris, 36
civil society, 79
Clinton, Hillary, 21, 105, 113, 114, 115
Coburn, Tom, 125
Coleman, Mary Sue, 53
communications
  cities as communications, 25, 86
  communications impact statements, 86
  community and, 25
  ISP, Internet service provider, 154, 155
  Net Neutrality, 154
  public access cable channels, 87
  urban planning relation to, 86
community organizing, 105, 106, 116
Congressional Budget Office, 125
Costco, 48, 156
creative class, 51, 115
creative communities, 86
Cronkite, Walter, 137
Crossett, Laura, 42
CVS, 182, 184
Davis, Andy, 83, 85, 143, 144
Davis, Edward, 184
Dean, John, 63
Declaration of Independence, 79, 94
Deeth, John, 57, 58
deferred gratification, 49
democracy
  Bureau of Democracy, Human Rights, and Labor, U.S. State Department, 5
  current world dictators, 5

Index – 191

deliberative democracy polling, 97
dictators, features of gaining and holding power, 6
dictators, features of gaining and holding power, evaluating Trump by, 9
dictators, focus on what doing not labels, 6
fundamental pillars of, 17
global war on democracy and human rights, 5
global war on democracy and human rights, what we can do, 11
human rights, 122
independent judiciary, 19
least worst of the alternatives, 84
libraries, 18
media, 18
percentage favoring alternative to democracy, by country, Pew Research Center, 5
percentage favoring alternatives to democracy, for U.S., Pew Research Center, 9
poverty, 22, 24
poverty, impact on life liberty and happiness, 79
poverty, working poor, 22
public education, 18
Russia Country Report on Human Rights, 5
voting, 23
voting rights, 19
voting, Voting Rights Act, 23
working class, 22
Dempsey, Martin, 165
Dickens, Charles, 25
disabilities, persons with accessibility for, 152
ADA, 145, 152
Douglass, Frederick power concedes nothing without a demand, 11
drugs

addicts, 66, 81
cocaine, 66
cocaine trade, 66
doping, 67
heroin, 66
illegal drugs, 65, 66
legalization, 66
marijuana, 66, 91
Olympics, PED use in first, 66
performance enhancing drugs (PED), 66
War on Drugs, 66, 67
economy
California's tuition-free college and economy, 44
can't gamble way to prosperity, 49
capitalism, 133, 135, 137
capitalism, and happiness, 80
capitalism, corruption in, 136
capitalism, monopoly, 154
capitalism, risks and rewards of, 132
capitalism, TIFs aberration in, 136
capitalism, TIFs as ideological hypocrisy in, 139
capitalism, TIFs not necessary in, 143
capitalism, we don't have, 136
circular economy, 97
comunism, 136
consumer spending 70% of, 81, 123, 128
corporatism, 80, 133, 136
education builds economy, 81
fascism, 136, 142
fascist economy, 137
global economy, 48, 52
Iowa needs college grads to create jobs, 34
Iowa, University of Iowa's contribution to, 33
linear economy, 97
local economy, 134
market economy, 135, 154
minimum wage, 82, 117

overseas markets,
  farmers loss of, 153
profit maximization,
  154
socialism, 105, 106,
  133, 135, 136, 137
working poor, shifting
  money from, 128
Edelen, Adam, 80
education
  Iowa City
    Community
    School Board, 72
  American Academy of
    Arts & Sciences, 52
  An Educational
    Compact for the
    21st Century, 52
  attacks on, ISIS-like
    destruction of
    treasure, 39
  Board of Regents,
    Iowa, 32, 43, 50, 55
  Board of Regents,
    Iowa, creating
    difficulties for UI
    President, 38
  Board of Regents,
    Iowa, criticism of UI
    President Sally
    Mason, 32

Board of Regents,
  Iowa, David
  Skorton and, 119
Board of Regents,
  Iowa, delegation of
  IPR operation, 46
Board of Regents,
  Iowa, democratic
  dialogue and, 35
Board of Regents,
  Iowa, emphasis on
  educating Iowans,
  47
Board of Regents,
  Iowa, failure to vet,
  38
Board of Regents,
  Iowa, IED along
  road to Iowa City
  left by, 33
Board of Regents,
  Iowa, Iowa Public
  Radio as part of, 46
Board of Regents,
  Iowa, legal
  challenges to
  process, 38
Board of Regents,
  Iowa, mission
  reassessment, 39

Index – 193

Board of Regents, Iowa, President, 37, 38
Board of Regents, Iowa, president selection process, 42
Board of Regents, Iowa, selection of UI President, 38
Board of Regents, Iowa, what is it with the, 32
community colleges, 52, 122
Engagement Tours, University of Iowa, 56
from K-12 to K-14, 51
Germany, Humboldt-Universitat, 47
Iowa Child Welfare Research Station, 31
Iowa City Community School Board, 26, 31, 73
Iowa State University, 55
Iowa State University, transfer of money to, 33
Iowa, failure to appreciate economic value of, 48
IPR, subsidiary of Board of Regents, Iowa, 46
James Leach, HUMANISTEAM, 54
K-12, 17, 31, 55, 71, 74
K-12, Iowa City Press-Citizen columns, 31, 72
K-12, Iowa Public Radio series on, 45
K-12, teachers' pay, 164
learning can be everywhere, 87
Lincoln Project, 52
Morill Act, 55
my interest in, 31
one-room schoolhouse, 51, 55
Outreach & Engagement Program, University of Iowa, 56
Parsons College, 42

Penn State, 64
private universities, 53
public education, 17, 18, 19, 51
public education, free, 47
Rutgers University, 64
School Board Advisory Board, 74
school board, open meetings, 26
school vouchers, 153
social studies, 156
tenure, centerpiece of academy, 39
tuition increases, 50
tuition-free college, 19, 36, 43, 51, 52, 54, 81, 117
tuition-free community college, 9 states with, 51
UCLA, 118
U-High, Iowa City, 31
University of California, Berkeley, 31, 43
University of Chicago, 63, 154
University of Iowa, 55, 68
University of Iowa College of Law, 31
University of Iowa, binge drinking students, 134
University of Iowa, Board of Regents and, 32
University of Iowa, child of, 52
University of Iowa, emergency preparedness, 77
University of Iowa, experimental schools, 31
University of Iowa, how Regents feel about, 34
University of Iowa, international students, 172
University of Iowa, Jim Throgmorton, 118
University of Iowa, mission reassessment, 40
University of Iowa, next president, 37
University of Iowa, Pentacrest, 146

University of Iowa, records of president selection process, 42
University of Iowa, students, stake in local politics, 148
University of Iowa, transfer of money from, 33
University of Maryland, 64
University of Missouri, 41
University of Northern Iowa, 55
University of Northern Iowa, transfer of money to, 33
University of Texas, Austin, 31
urban and regional planning, 118
Eisenhower, Dwight, 159, 162
environment
  composting, 149
  corporate pollution, 154
  landfills, 149
  LEED certification, 152
  recycling, 96, 97, 149
Ernst, Joni, 112
FCC, ii, 18, 61, 90
  broadcasters employment of African Americans, 91
  commissioner, 45, 85
  educational radio licenses, 46
  Fairness Doctrine, 18
  first woman commissioner, 45
  Net Neutrality, 18, 154, 155
  universities' broadcast licenses are for educational purposes, 45
Felt, Mark, 89
Ferlinghetti, Lawrence, 20, 25, 84
Fethke, Gary, 33
Finland, 47
football, 60, 64, 178
  assumption of risk, 67
  athletic directors, 64
  brain injuries, 67
  coach, fired for falsifying resume, 38

Index – 197

college football, 63, 136
college football, alcohol as fun factor, 71
college football, alcohol industry, 64
college football, big money, 60, 63, 64, 65, 70
college football, gambling industry, 64
college football, gambling industry, Riverside gambling casino, 71
college football, impact on neighborhood, 71
enhanced performance, 67, 68
football corporations, 65
football critics, 63
game day experience, 68, 70, 71
Green Bay Packers, 60
Hawkeyes, 65, 69, 70, 71
health care costs, 64
high school, 60
Kinnick Stadium, 65, 68, 69, 71
level playing field, 67, 68
most violent sport, 160
NCAA, 63, 64, 65, 71
NFL, 60, 61, 62, 65, 70, 71, 136
only a game, 62
season tickets, cost of, 69, 70
small college, 60
sports science, 67
Super Bowl, 61
TV show, 62
University of Missouri, team boycott, 41
Ford, Gerald, 163
forgiveness
 how much is forgivable in others, 100
Fox News, 127
France, 47
Franklin, Benjamin, 15
Friedman, Milton, 154
Frost, David, 101
Garland, Merrick, 107, 109

Gekko, Gordon, 137
Georges-Picot,
   Francois, 172
Germany, 47, 48, 81,
   118
   economic benefits of
      education, 48
   German students, 48
   global economy, 48
   Länders, 48
   tuition free education,
      47
   tuition free education,
      49
   world citizens, 48
Glass-Steagall, 43
Goebbels, Joseph, 104
Goodrum, Ian, 179, 181
governance
   boards, 43, 74
   boards, principles, 39
Grassley, Charles, 56,
   108, 112
hamburgers, five-step
   program to increase
   sales, 69
happiness, 79, 80
Harreld, Bruce
   and Educational
      Compact, 53
   and University of
      Missouri, 41
   archive of presidency,
      42
   asked to transition UI,
      39
   critics embrace status
      quo, 37
   falsified resume, 38
   lack of academic
      experience, 38
   no resignation of, 38
   objections to selection
      of, 37
   PAC proposal, 54
   qualifications, 40
   quotes, 53, 55
   Regents could have
      picked without
      process, 38
   selection involved
      special treatment,
      38
Harvey, Paul, 137
health care
   Cancer Moonshot, 87,
      88
   carcinogens, 88, 89,
      90
   Genomic Data
      Commons, 88
   health care costs, 64,
      81, 95

legal or moral obligation to care for others, 93
public health, DWD, driving while distracted, 156
public health, DWI, driving while intoxicated, 157
public health, DWT, driving while texting, 155
public health, guns in homes threat to owner, 161
public health, guns, drugs and, 66
public health, guns, kill more every day than most school shootings, 181
public health, guns, more deaths every month than from 9/11, 174
public health, Harvard School of Public Health, 97
public health, sanitation and clean water, 88, 99
public health, seat belts, 97
right, or product, and privilege, 94
universal single-payer, 48, 81, 117
who profits from causing cancer, 89
Heldt, Diane, 45
Hennock, Frieda, 45
Hoover, Herbert, 162
housing
  homeless, 78, 81
  impact on communication, 86
humanitarianism, 122
Hutchins, Robert Maynard, 63
income inequality, 62, 80, 121, 127
Inside Scientology, Janet Reitman, 182
International Monetary Fund, 124
Iowa City
  Academy of Arts & Sciences, 53
  architectural gems of, 145
  assets, 146
  basic data and information, 10

City Council, 118
City Council, and bar owners, 59
City Council, downtown, 146
City Council, election, 20
City Council, generous to bar owners, 57
City Council, Marc Moen and, 83
City Council, sales taxes, 127
City Council, Throgmorton, Jim and, 118
City Council, TIFs, 143, 144
City of Literature, 179
city's 1%, developers and business owners, 119
Civil War cottages, 83
consensus regarding destruction of old and building new, 85
consensus, need for, 82
Coral Ridge Mall, 83
downtown and mall, 83
downtown laid out 1839, 82
economic and cultural magnet, 144
historic preservation, 84
Historic Preservation Commission, 83
Houston once size of, 144
northern racism, 23
northern racism, now less, 25
Old Capitol, 145, 146, 149
Regents, why business should support, 55
residents deserve to be heard, 119
Throgmorton, Jim, 118
TIFs, 144
unlike Washington, D.C., 147
voter registration, percentage of those eligible, 20
Iowa Ideas, 122
Iowa Legislature

can't pass laugh test, 52
education, emphasis on educating Iowans, 47
Iowa nice, 71
Iowa Public Radio
  delegation from Regents, 46
  failure to use to explain higher education, 44
  government body, 45, 46
  Jerald Schnoor's programs, failure to carry, 44
  multi-million-dollar statewide network, 56
  neither educational nor noncommercial, 46
  not a government body, 46
  not non-commercial, 46
  subsidiary of licensees, 46
Iowa Workforce Development, 48
Iran, 171
Iraq, 111, 160, 164, 165, 166, 167, 171, 176, 178
  antiquities, 39
IRS, 125
ISIS, 111, 165, 166, 176, 177, 180, 181
Jay, John, 21, 127
Jefferson, Thomas, 17, 18
Jesus, 94, 122
Johnson County
  Administration Building, 146
  County Board of Supervisors, 139
  County Board of Supervisors, need public approval for bonds, 152
  County Board of Supervisors, Rettig, Janelle, 119
  courthouse, 145, 146, 147, 148, 149, 150, 151
  courthouse annex bond proposal, 151
Johnson, Jeh C., 166
Johnson, Lyndon, 23, 96
Jordan, 171

Jordan, Erin, 125
Kansas City, 41, 118
King, Steve, 112
Kipling, Rudyard, 95
Koch brothers, 38
Kohut, Andrew, 168
Landon, Alf, 54
Lao Tsu, 25
law
  constitution, Declaration of War, Art. I, Sec. 8, Cl. 11, 1
  defamation, 72, 73, 101
  drug courts, 81
  drug treatment court, 152
  First Amendment, 18, 29, 73
  incarceration avoidance, 148
  independent judiciary, 19
  New York Times v. Sullivan, 73
  prisons, for-profit, 42
  prisons, mandatory minimums, 81
  reasonable and proper, early Iowa speed limit, 156
social norms, 72
U.S. Court of Appeals, 5th Circuit, 90
Leach, James, 53, 54
Lebanon, 171
Lehrer, Tom
  National Brotherhood Week, lyrics, 7
Liepman, Andrew, 166
Lincoln, Abraham, 52, 55
Los Angeles, 82, 118
Louisiana, 51
Louisville, 118
Maddow, Rachel, 106
Madison, James, 18
Marcus, Danielle, 184
Mason, Sally, 32
McCain, John, 113
McConnell, Mitch, 108, 109
McGinness, Jeff, 100
McVeigh, Timothy, 184
Mearns, Hughes, 135
media reform movement, 85
Mediacom, 154
Menino, Thomas M., 183
Midwest Academy, 116
Miller, Vanessa, 77

Mitchell, Joni, 17
Moen, Marc, 83, 84
Montgomery Ward, 82
Motivated Numeracy and Enlightened Self-Government, 104
Moynihan, Daniel, 104
MSNBC, 106
multi-tasking, 157
museums
   Museum of Art, University of Iowa, 53
Myers, Vernā, 93
Nader, Ralph, 156
Nash, Ogden, 69
National Endowment for the Humanities, 53
National Historic Places, U.S. Register of, 146, 149, 152
National Institute for Occupational Safety and Health, 89
National Rifle Association, 78, 161
Neff, John, 57
Net Neutrality, 18
Never Happen Again, 77
New York, 21, 51, 54, 81, 104, 174
economic growth and education, 49
New York Times, 35, 73, 182
NFL, 60
Nixon, Richard, 63, 101
Norquist, Grover, 42, 122, 124
Norway, 47
Obama, Barack, 35, 48, 49, 91, 105, 106, 107, 108, 111, 116, 165, 167, 180
I've been a community organizer, 116
Occupy, 106
Oklahoma
   Dust Bowl, 49
Oklahoma City, 184
Olsen, Matthew, 166
Oregon, 51
original meaning, 108
Ottoman Empire, 172
Oxford English Dictionary, 20
Parsons, Dave, 147
Pew Research Center, 168
Philadelphia, 159
Physicians for Social Responsibility, 89

Planned Parenthood, 41
politics
  campaign contributions, 50, 52, 110, 117, 125, 126, 162
  campaign contributions, rate of return on, 124
  campaign contributors, 94, 117
  Democratic Party, 124
  Democratic Party, turn toward Wall Street, 54
  education, like Democratic Party, neglectful of constituents, 54
  FDR, coalition, key to victory, 54
  FDR, support of unemployed, 54
  FDR, support of union members, 54
  FDR, support of working class, 54
  FDR, support of working poor, 54
  Green Party, 118
  Libertarian, 118
  lobbying, 50
  PACs, 56, 117
  PACs, pro-education, 54
  public citizen, 156
  Republcan Party, 23, 112, 113, 115, 124
  Republican Party, 124
  Teapot Dome, 153
  voters, 17, 18, 19, 20, 21, 22, 59, 81, 84, 102, 132, 139, 143, 148, 156
  voters, Democrats search for on east and left coasts, 54
  voters, limits on access to information, 110
  voters, percentage who register, by countries, 123
  voters, restrictions on, 108
Pope Francis, 80, 104
Portugal, 66, 68
positions and interests, difference between, 148
Public Policy

Safe, Equitable and Thriving Communities Task Force, Cedar Rapids, 24
public schools, 18
Putin, Vladimir, 35, 36
  3 million questions, 37
  acknowledged challenges, 35
  answers questions, 36
  Bruce Rastetter, things to discuss with, 36
  example of democratic dialogue for Rastetter offered by, 35
  firmer grasp of American politics than Rastetter, 36
  four hour call-in show, 36
  live call-in show, 35
  quick solutions, 36
  responsiveness, 36
  takes questions from constituents, 36
  years with KGB, 35

Quayle, Dan, 105
quotations and expressions
  a cancer growing on the presidency, 63
  A crucial principle is at stake...the deliberative process, 107
  a people who mean to be their own Governors, must arm themselves with the power which knowledge gives, 18
  a picture is worth a thousand words, 182
  a Republic if you can keep it, 15
  alcohol does for football fans what bacon does for hamburger, 69
  and that's the way it is, 137
  because you have to start somewhere, 100
  believing is seeing, 104, 135

best practices, 118
candy is dandy/but liquor is quicker, 70
consultants borrow your watch tell you the time then walk off with your watch, 32
do the wrong thing better, 137, 141
drain the swamp, 153
drink responsibly, 134
every night before it goes to bed television gets down on its knees and prays to war, 161
everyone is entitled to his own opinion, but not to his own facts, 104
follow the money, 89
fool me once, shame on you; fool me twice, shame on me, 102
full Grassley, 56
get 'er done, 148, 151
getting to yes, 148, 151
give the people a voice, 108
goal is to get government down to the size where we can drown it in the bathtub, 42, 122, 124
Goldilocks' porridge tasting, 150
government is the problem, 139
greed is good, 80, 137
he that filches from me my good name Robs me of that which not enriches him And makes me poor indeed, 100
hope is not a strategy, 53
how would we know if we ever were successful, 155, 167
I am waiting for someone to really discover America, 20, 84
I built that, 80

I can't work in a home that keeps an alligator in the bathtub, 78
I could be the first presidential candidate to run and make money on it, 112
I don't care who does the electing just so long as I get to do the nominating, 21
I don't like surprises, 78
I don't shove worth a damn, 96
I follow you all but the therefore, 149, 150
I follow you all but the therefore, 59
if it looks, walks, and quacks like a duck, 37, 47
if you repeat a lie often enough, people will believe it, 104
if you think education's expensive try paying for ignorance, 44
Iowa can't gamble its way to prosperity, 49
Iowa nice, 114
it's not what we don't know that's the problem, it's what we know that ain't so, 104
I've got mine Jack, 80
last night I saw upon the stair a little man who wasn't there, 135
level playing field, 68
making the haystack bigger doesn't make the needle easier to find, 174
millions of Americans fighting to transform our country, 117
mission accomplished, 168
nobody knew that it could be so complicated, 93
oh look at the squirrel, 121

our oil has found its way under someone else's land, 165
Plan B, 53, 166
privatize profits and socialize losses, 142
put down the books of Ayn Rand and pick up the books of Matthew, Mark, Luke and John, 80
Robin Hood in reverse, 128
sixty seconds worth of distance run, 95
small boy with hammer thiinks everything needs pounding, 168
tax policy is about benefitting the political class and the well-connected and the well-heeled, 125
taxes are just another way to buy stuff we need, 129

that's my story and I'm sticking to it, 149
the least of these, 94, 122, 123
the only winning move is not to play, 144, 168, 173
the rest of the story, 137
they do talk about my language, right?, 112
this is not about me, it's about we, 117
this must never happen again, 78
those who own the country ought to govern it, 21, 127
tie your reform to the tail of greed, and watch it run off down the street, 96
TINA, there is no alternative, 149, 151
too big to jail, 127
we owe the people something back, 55
were it left to me to decide whether we

should have a government without newspapers, or newspapers without a government, I should not hesitate a moment to prefer the latter, 18
we're number one, 160
what did you do with the last nickel I gave you, 163
what have you done for us lately, 55
whatever is the question war is not the answer, 173
whatever is your first priority your second priority has to be media reform, 86
when his [good leader's] work is done the people will say we did this ourselves, 25
when the President does it, that means it is not illegal, 101
white privilege, 92
why will coal mine owners have less ability to maintain coal miners unsafe working conditions than they do now, 116
winning isn't everything, it's the only thing, 103
you don't know what you've got until it's gone, 17, 131
you get what you measure, 34, 96
what you incentivize, 96
you may not get any pay, but at least you get a lot of grief, 74
racism
   Confederate flags, 91
   cultural diversity, 93
   disparity
      arrests, car/home purchases, health care, jobs, prison, 91
   impact on black children, 92

now more prison laborers, than once were slaves, 66
poll tax, 23, 90
south, 1950s, consequences of, 90
Southern Poverty Law Center, 91
underground railroad, 23
Rastetter, Bruce, 35, 36, 37
  desire to transition UI, 39
  potential discussion questions with Putin, 36
  Putin example of rapid response to democratic dialogue, 36
  transitioning enterprises through change, 40
Ray, Robert D., 170, 172
Reagan, Ronald, 107
Reitman, Janet, 182
Republican Party, 107, 112, 113, 114, 115
Rettig, Janelle, 119, 120
Reynolds, Kim, 50
Rhode Island, 51
Rolling Stone magazine, 182, 183, 184
Romney, Mitt, 113
Roosevelt, Franklin D., 54
Roosevelt, Teddy, 63
rugged individualism, 122
Russia, 171, 172, 173
Russia, provision of tuition-free college, 36
Ryan, Paul, 113
Sanders, Bernie, 81, 113, 115, 116, 117, 118
Saudi Arabia, 171
Scalia, Antonin, 107, 108
Schnoor, Jerald L., 44
Scrooge, Ebenezer, 25
Sears, 82
Sierra Club, 95
Skorton, David, 32, 119
Slovenia, 47
Smithsonian Institution, 32
Snopes, 104, 105, 106
Social Security, 125
South Dakota, 51

Stewart, Jon, 128
Sullivan, Rod, 139
Supreme Court, 72, 107, 108, 127
Sweden, 47, 123
Swift, Jonathan, 124
  solution for poor children eat them, 124
Sykes, Mark, 172
Syria, 165
Tammany Hall, 21
taxes
  can't tax cut way to prosperity, 49
  employers' taxes, 121
  gasoline taxes, 121, 129, 130, 131
  mileage tax, 129
  sales taxes, 121, 125, 126, 127, 128
  tax breaks, 52, 80, 124, 125, 126, 128, 140
  tax code, 123, 142
  tax cuts, 48, 94, 99, 121, 123
  tax deduction, 84
  tax policy, 121, 125
  tax reform, 17
  tax savings, 80
  tax talk, 123

TIF, 101, 133, 134, 139, 140, 141, 143, 144
TIF, applying lipstick to, 144
TIF, as tax break, 126
TIF, campaign contributions, exchange for, 126
TIF, can be as addictive as alcohol, 134
TIF, checklist before granting, 141
TIF, City Council meeting, 84
TIF, diversion of tax revenue, 139
TIF, do not require public approval, 152
TIF, example of corporatism, 133
TIF, fault of government not recipient, 84
TIF, given over taxpayers' objections, 132
TIF, here to stay, 132
TIF, high risk, 133

TIF, like death and taxes, 132
TIF, market distortion, 133
TIF, need for questioned, 133
TIF, often fail, 133
TIF, originally for low income housing, 132
TIF, other government tools more effective, 133
TIF, over 40 blog posts, 121
TIF, playing Santa with others' money, 132
TIF, rob other programs, 133
TIF, should require public approval, 132
TIF, taxpayer funding of private ventures, 83
TIF, TIF Towers, 126
TIF, unfair to competitors, 140
working poor, rates higher than for wealthy, 128

Tea Party, 106
TED talks, 92
television
  ABC, 61
  HDTV, 61
Tennessee, 48, 51
  education, tuition free community college, 49
Texas, 23, 31, 50, 90
Thatcher, Margaret, 149
Throgmorton, Jim, 118, 142, 143
Time magazine
  Person of the Year, Hitler, Stalin, 183
tobacco, 62, 89
  addiction, 82
  industry hooks junior high kids, 89
Trump, Donald, 18, 35, 36, 50, 93, 110, 111, 112, 113, 114, 115, 153, 154
Tsarnaev, Dzhokhar (Jahar), 182, 183, 184
Turkey, 171
Twain, Mark, 104
Tweed, William "Boss", 21
unions, 43

military prevention of organizing, 162
unionize, 64
United Nations
 Office of the High Commissioner Human Rights, 122
 Statement on Visit to the USA on Extreme Poverty and Human Rights, 122
 Universal Declaration of Human Rights, 26, 48
urban legends, 105
Valentine, Crystal, 92
veterans, 26, 162
 GI Bill, 51, 81
 workforce of, 51
video games, 21, 64
Waddington, Lynda, 122
Wag the Dog, 165
Walgreens, 182, 184
Wall Street, 21, 54, 117, 137
Walmart, 156
Walsh, Joe, 93, 94
war

9/11, Saudis not Afghans responsible, 2, 175
Afghanistan War, what we learned from the, 172
al Qaeda, 166
Albania, threat of war from, movie Wag the Dog, 165
answer, whatever is the question war is not the answer, 173
avoiding war, six step program for, 168
campaign donors support for, 163
cheerleaders for war, media as, 160
computers as weapons, Internet as battlefield, 4
costs, $trillions of debt on credit card, 3, 160
costs, Afghanistan and Iraq, estimates $1-5 trillion, 164
costs, audits are impossible, 163
costs, caring for wounded, 164

costs, General Accounting Office, 163
costs, one attack equaled 1700 teachers' pay, 164
costs, opportunity costs, 160, 164
costs, paying for war, supplementary war tax, 169
costs, U.S. spends more than next 9 nations combined, 160
cyber attacks, 164
Department of Veterans Affairs, 164
draft, 168
ethical, legal and social issues (ELSI), 169
exit strategy, what is our, 167
global thermonuclear war, War Games movie, 168
go shopping, post 9/11 presidential advice was to, 169
goal, what is our, 166, 167
guns, homes with, 161
guns, U.S. gun death rate 20 times world average, 161
Insurrection Act, 162
involvement in, increases likelihood we'll be attacked, 166
Iraq War, what we learned from the, 172
Iraq, doubling of U.S. troops in, 167
Iraq, not rational target post 9/11, 173
ISIL, no evidence planning to attack homeland, 166
ISIS, emerges after al Qaeda, 166
ISIS, goal to degrade and destroy, 166
ISIS, goal to terrorize us not take our homeland, 175

ISIS, has proven creative and adaptable, 180
ISIS, Syria, U.S. leaves youth no option but to join ISIS, 176
Islamic State, increases recruitment of terrorists by, 168
mass violence, young angry Americans, must treat anger before have to treat victims, 180
military leaders, caution and rational analysis of, 165
military, U.S in 150 countries, 2
military, use of to control civilians, 162
military-industrial complex, 116, 159, 162, 165
Muslims, focus on, President Obama unconstitutional and inhospitable, 180

national anthem celebrates war, 160
National Counterterrorism Center, 166
Navy Pre-Flight Training School, Iowa City, 2
NSA, 162
Pearl Harbor, 1
perpetual wars, 43, 159, 160
police, militarization of, 160
political support for, 161, 163
political support for, as first rather than last resort, like small boy with hammer, 168
political support for, intelligence community less alarmist, 166
Posse Comitatus Act, 162
Powell Doctrine, questions to ask before going to war, 169

preemptive wars, 160, 166
public, little inclination of, to deal with, 168
rethinking U.S. approach to, 167
revenge, war not most effective, 167
Saudi Arabia, more logical target than Afghanistan post 9/11, 173
survivors, left to fend for themselves, 167
Syria, adding of to expanding battlefield, 165
Syria, al Qaeda in, 171
Syria, Arab Spring, demonstrators fired on, 171
Syria, Free Syrian Army, 171
Syria, Hezbollah in, 171
Syria, ISIS in, 171
Syria, Kurds in, 171
Syria, numbers of dead, refugees, 171
Syria, refugees, 173
Syria, refugees, ban of makes ISIS stronger, 175
Syria, war in, 171
terrorism is not a nation, 173
terrorism, advance warnings, failure to heed, 174
terrorism, and risk assessment, 173
terrorism, Boston bombing, 4, 182
terrorism, death from attack compared with other causes, 173
terrorism, difficulties in fighting, 3
terrorism, evidence we're terrorised strengthens terrorists, 178
terrorism, ISIS Paris attacks, 174
terrorism, ISIS, advises followers just do the killing, 181
terrorism, issues involving, 159

terrorism, like whack-a-mole, the more we kill the more they recruit, 178
terrorism, Muslims, Christians committed more terrorist attacks than, 174
terrorism, NSA surveillance, 174
terrorism, terrorists have won when football fans xrayed, 176
terrorism, terrorists need evidence of West's war on Islam, 177
terrorism, Tsarnaev on Rolling Stone cover, 182
terrorism, what is terrorists ultimate goal, 176
terrorism, response to, 173
terrorists' bombs, 164
video games, 161
Viet Nam war, 168
Viet Nam War, what we learned from the, 172
War Games movie, 168
wars of choice, 159
World War I, 1
World War II, 175
World War II, GI Bill, economic growth from, 49
World War II, post-war economic boom, 51
World War II, post-war economy, 81
World War II, post-war, veterans, GI Bill, tuition-free college, 54
World War II, preparing to fight it again, 163
World War II, U.S. refusal of German Jewish refugees, 175
World War II, won in four years, 168
World War II, won in four years, compare perpetual wars, 159

World War II, citizen
    sacrifice, 168
World War III is not
    World War II, 173
World War III, Syria
    war as regional
    version of, 171
world, militarization of
    by U.S., 160
Washington, D.C., 147,
    151
waste
  bottle deposits, 97
  landfills, zero waste
    tp, 97
  showers, 96
  those who profit from
    wastefulness, 97
  turn off lights, 96
  wasted, meaning of,
    95
water
  100,000 toxic
    substances
    untested, 98
  agricultural use, 98
  Flint, Michigan, 98
  lead in, 98
  life began in, 98
  ocean levels rising,
    99
  water wars, 96, 99
Watergate, 63, 88
  Mark Felt, 89
White House, 22, 63,
    87, 153
White, James A., 92
Williams, Mason, 160
Wise, Phyllis, 53
Wolfe, Timothy M., 41
Woodward, Bob, 88
Yale, 104
Yarrow, Peter, 33
Young, David, 112

Made in the USA
Lexington, KY
17 December 2019